VISITORS' ATLAS & GUIDE

A-Z DEV CORNWALL
WEST SOMERSET

CONTENTS

Geographers' A-Z Map Company Ltd

Head Office : (General Enquiries & Trade Sales)
Fairfield Road, Borough Green, Sevenoaks,
Kent TN15 8PP Telephone: 01732 781000

Showrooms : (Retail Sales)
44 Gray's Inn Road, London, WC1X 8HX
Telephone: 020 7440 9500

www.a-zmaps.co.uk

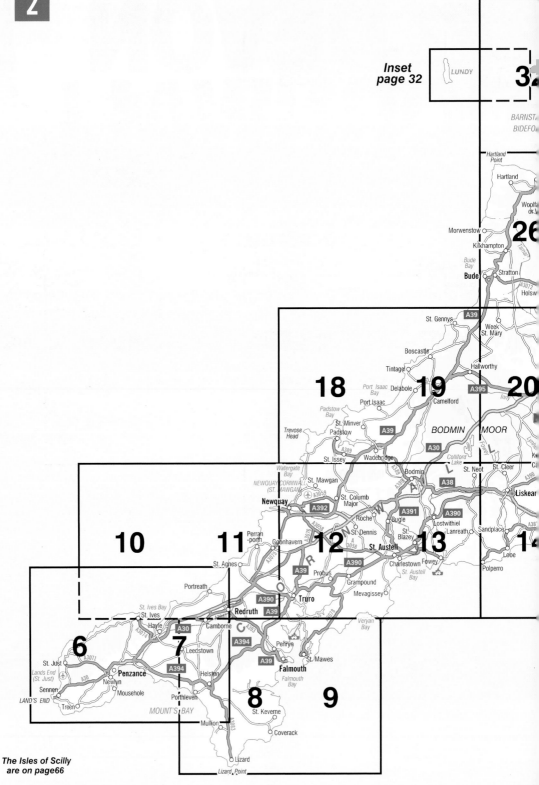

2

Inset
page 32

LUNDY

32

BARNST
BIDEFO

*Hartland
Point*

Hartland

Woolfa
or W

Morwenstow

26

Kilkhampton

Tamar

*Bude
Bay*

Stratton

Bude

A3072

Holsw

St. Gennys

A39

Week
St. Mary

Boscastle

Hallworthy

Tintagel

18

*Port Isaac
Bay*

Delabole

19

A395

20

Port Isaac

Camelford

*Padstow
Bay*

St. Minver

A39

BODMIN   MOOR

*Trevose
Head*

Padstow

A389

*Colliford
Lake*

Ke

St. Issey

Wadebridge

St. Neot

St. Cleer

Ca

*Watergate
Bay*

Bodmin

A30

A38

Liskear

*NEWQUAY CORNWALL
(ST. MAWGAN)*

St. Mawgan

St. Columb
Major

A391

A390

Lanreath

Sandplace

10

11

A3058

St. Dennis

St.
Blazey

13

Looe

14

Perran
-porth

Goonhavern

12

A3058

St. Austell

Fowey

Polperro

St. Agnes

Charlestown

*St. Austell
Bay*

Portreath

Probus

Grampound

St. Ives Bay

St. Ives

Redruth

A390

A39

Mevagissey

*Veryan
Bay*

Hayle

A30

Camborne

A394

Truro

6

7

Leedstown

A394

A39

Penryn

St. Mawes

St. Just

Helston

Falmouth

St. Just)

Penzance

*Falmouth
Bay*

9

*Lands End
(St. Just)*

Newlyn

8

Sennen

A30

Mousehole

Porthleven

Treen

St. Keverne

LAND'S END

MOUNT'S BAY

Mullion

A3083

Coverack

**The Isles of Scilly
are on page66**

Lizard

Lizard Point

BRISTOL CHANNEL

THE VALE OF GLAMORGAN

Ogmore-by-Sea · Cowbridge · A48 · Dinas Powys
Wick · A4050 · Penarth · Clevedon · CORDANO · 20 · BRISTOL
Llantwit Major · Barry · Nailsea · Yatton

WESTON-SUPER-MARE · 21 · A370 · Congresbury · Blagdon · 3
Brean · Bleadon · Wins · Cheddar · Wes Harptr · Che
East Brent · SEDGEMOOR · A38 · Draycott · Wells
Burnham-on-Sea · Wedmore · Westbury-sub-Mendip
Highbridge · Mark · Meare · A36 · Glastonbury

33 Ilfracombe · Combe Martin · Lynton · Porlock Bay · Porlock · Minehead · **35** · Watchet · **36** · Washford · **37**
Parracombe · A39 · EXMOOR · Dunster · Nether Stowey · Cannington · BRIDGWATER
Bittadon · Simonsbath · Timbercombe · Holford · Bridgwater · Westonzoyland
Braunton · Exford · Wheddon Cross · BRENDON HILLS · Williton · North Petherton · Othery
Barnstaple · Withypool · Winsford · Brompton Regis · SOMERSET · QUANTOCK HILLS
A361 · North Molton · Dulverton · Wiveliscombe · Bishop's Lydeard · TAUNTON · Langport · Somerton
Bideford · South Molton · Bampton · Norton Fitzwarren · A358 · South Petherton
Atherington · Chulmleigh · Witheridge · Tiverton · Wellington · TAUNTON DEANE · Corfe · Ilminster · Martock
Great Torrington · Chawleigh · Cullompton · Hemyock · A303 · Merriott · East Chinnock
27 · Dolton · **28** · Bickleigh · **29** · A361 · **30** · Culmstock · **31** · Winsham · Crewkerne
A386 · Winkleigh · Copplestone · Uffculme · Yarcombe · Chard · Broadwindsor
Highampton · Hatherleigh · Bow · Crediton · A30 · Axminster · Beaminster
Exbourne · Okehampton · Broadclyst · Honiton · Bridport
21 · **22** · EXETER · Ottery St. Mary · Colyton · Lyme Regis · A35
Bridestowe · Chagford · Moretonhampstead · Sidbury · Beer · Seaton · Burton Bradstock
Two Bridges · Widecombe in the Moor · Topsham · Sidmouth · LYME BAY · Abbotsbury
DARTMOOR · Bovey Tracey · **23** · Budleigh Salterton · **24** · **25**
Tavistock · Princetown · Dartmeet · Ashburton · Chudleigh · EXMOUTH
Horrabridge · Buckfastleigh · Kingsteignton · Dawlish
PLYMOUTH · Lee Moor · Newton Abbot · Teignmouth · Kingskerswell
Plympton · Ivybridge · A380 · TORQUAY
15 · Yealmpton · **16** · Avonwick · Totnes · PAIGNTON · **17** · Brixham
Plymstock · Modbury · Halwell · Dartmouth · Kingswear
Newton Ferrers · Kingston · Loddiswell · Start Bay
Bigbury Bay · Thurlestone · Kingsbridge · Torcross
Salcombe · Start Point

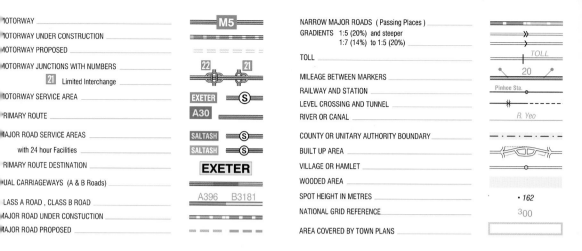

MOTORWAY

MOTORWAY UNDER CONSTRUCTION

MOTORWAY PROPOSED

MOTORWAY JUNCTIONS WITH NUMBERS

21 Limited Interchange

MOTORWAY SERVICE AREA

PRIMARY ROUTE

MAJOR ROAD SERVICE AREAS

with 24 hour Facilities

PRIMARY ROUTE DESTINATION

DUAL CARRIAGEWAYS (A & B Roads)

CLASS A ROAD , CLASS B ROAD

MAJOR ROAD UNDER CONSTUCTION

MAJOR ROAD PROPOSED

M5

22   21

EXETER ══S

A30

SALTASH ══S

SALTASH ══S

EXETER

A396   B3181

NARROW MAJOR ROADS (Passing Places)
GRADIENTS 1:5 (20%) and steeper
               1:7 (14%) to 1:5 (20%)

TOLL

MILEAGE BETWEEN MARKERS

RAILWAY AND STATION

LEVEL CROSSING AND TUNNEL

RIVER OR CANAL

COUNTY OR UNITARY AUTHORITY BOUNDARY

BUILT UP AREA

VILLAGE OR HAMLET

WOODED AREA

SPOT HEIGHT IN METRES

NATIONAL GRID REFERENCE

AREA COVERED BY TOWN PLANS

TOLL

20

Pinhoe Sta.

R. Yeo

• 162

300

TOURIST INFORMATION

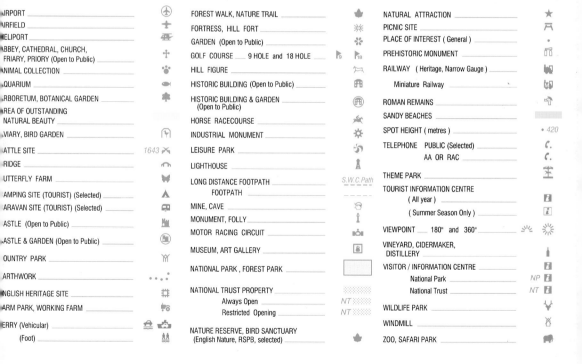

AIRPORT

AIRFIELD

HELIPORT

ABBEY, CATHEDRAL, CHURCH,
FRIARY, PRIORY (Open to Public)

ANIMAL COLLECTION

AQUARIUM

ARBORETUM, BOTANICAL GARDEN

AREA OF OUTSTANDING
NATURAL BEAUTY

AVIARY, BIRD GARDEN

BATTLE SITE   1643

BRIDGE

BUTTERFLY FARM

CAMPING SITE (TOURIST) (Selected)

CARAVAN SITE (TOURIST) (Selected)

CASTLE (Open to Public)

CASTLE & GARDEN (Open to Public)

COUNTRY PARK

EARTHWORK

ENGLISH HERITAGE SITE

FARM PARK, WORKING FARM

FERRY (Vehicular)

        (Foot)

FOREST WALK, NATURE TRAIL

FORTRESS, HILL FORT

GARDEN (Open to Public)

GOLF COURSE   9 HOLE and 18 HOLE

HILL FIGURE

HISTORIC BUILDING (Open to Public)

HISTORIC BUILDING & GARDEN
   (Open to Public)

HORSE RACECOURSE

INDUSTRIAL MONUMENT

LEISURE PARK

LIGHTHOUSE

LONG DISTANCE FOOTPATH   S.W.C.Path
          FOOTPATH

MINE, CAVE

MONUMENT, FOLLY

MOTOR RACING CIRCUIT

MUSEUM, ART GALLERY

NATIONAL PARK , FOREST PARK

NATIONAL TRUST PROPERTY
   Always Open   NT
   Restricted Opening   NT

NATURE RESERVE, BIRD SANCTUARY
   (English Nature, RSPB, selected)

NATURAL ATTRACTION

PICNIC SITE

PLACE OF INTEREST (General)

PREHISTORIC MONUMENT

RAILWAY (Heritage, Narrow Gauge)

   Miniature Railway

ROMAN REMAINS

SANDY BEACHES

SPOT HEIGHT (metres)   • 420

TELEPHONE   PUBLIC (Selected)
              AA OR RAC

THEME PARK

TOURIST INFORMATION CENTRE
   (All year)
   (Summer Season Only)

VIEWPOINT   180° and 360°

VINEYARD, CIDERMAKER,
   DISTILLERY

VISITOR / INFORMATION CENTRE
              National Park   NP
              National Trust   NT

WILDLIFE PARK

WINDMILL

ZOO, SAFARI PARK

: 158,400

SCALE

2.5 Miles to 1 Inch
1.584 Kms (0.98 Miles) to 1 cm

0   1   2   3   4   5   10 Miles

0   1   2   3   4   5   10   15 Kilometres

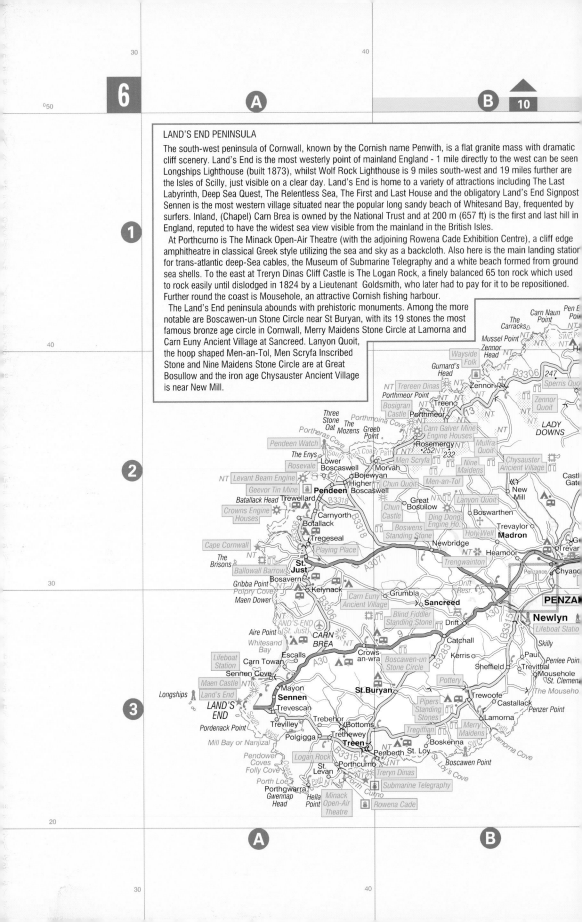

LAND'S END PENINSULA

The south-west peninsula of Cornwall, known by the Cornish name Penwith, is a flat granite mass with dramatic cliff scenery. Land's End is the most westerly point of mainland England - 1 mile directly to the west can be seen Longships Lighthouse (built 1873), whilst Wolf Rock Lighthouse is 9 miles south-west and 19 miles further are the Isles of Scilly, just visible on a clear day. Land's End is home to a variety of attractions including The Last Labyrinth, Deep Sea Quest, The Relentless Sea, The First and Last House and the obligatory Land's End Signpost Sennen is the most western village situated near the popular long sandy beach of Whitesand Bay, frequented by surfers. Inland, (Chapel) Carn Brea is owned by the National Trust and at 200 m (657 ft) is the first and last hill in England, reputed to have the widest sea view visible from the mainland in the British Isles.

At Porthcurno is The Minack Open-Air Theatre (with the adjoining Rowena Cade Exhibition Centre), a cliff edge amphitheatre in classical Greek style utilizing the sea and sky as a backcloth. Also here is the main landing station for trans-atlantic deep-Sea cables, the Museum of Submarine Telegraphy and a white beach formed from ground sea shells. To the east at Treryn Dinas Cliff Castle is The Logan Rock, a finely balanced 65 ton rock which used to rock easily until dislodged in 1824 by a Lieutenant Goldsmith, who later had to pay for it to be repositioned. Further round the coast is Mousehole, an attractive Cornish fishing harbour.

The Land's End peninsula abounds with prehistoric monuments. Among the more notable are Boscawen-un Stone Circle near St Buryan, with its 19 stones the most famous bronze age circle in Cornwall, Merry Maidens Stone Circle at Lamorna and Carn Euny Ancient Village at Sancreed. Lanyon Quoit, the hoop shaped Men-an-Tol, Men Scryfa Inscribed Stone and Nine Maidens Stone Circle are at Great Bosullow and the iron age Chysauster Ancient Village is near New Mill.

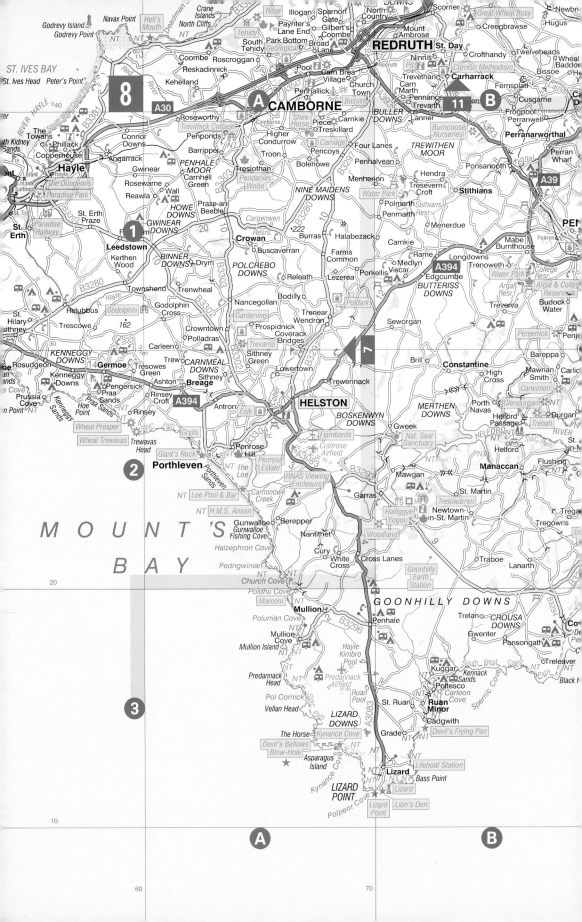

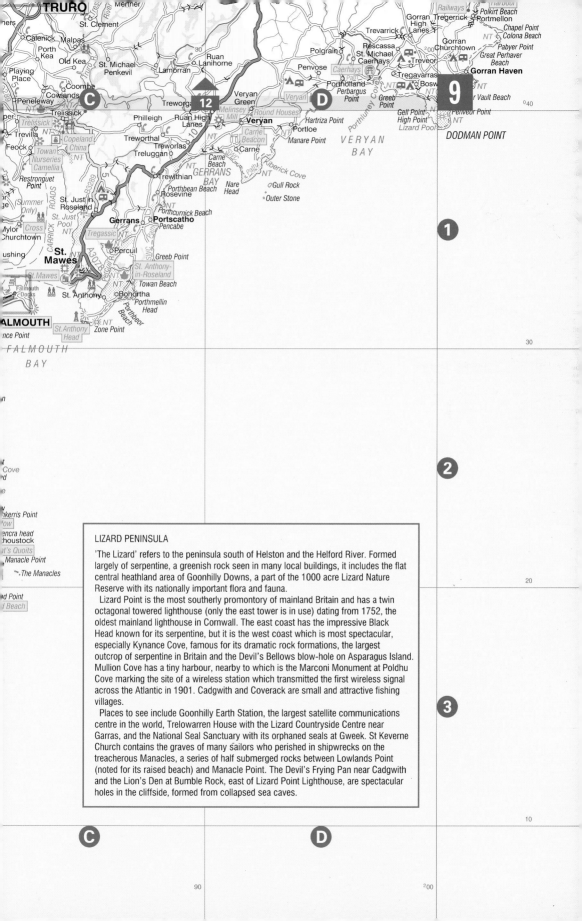

TRURO
Merther
St. Clement
Calenick   Malpas
Porth
Kea   Old Kea   St. Michael
Penkevil
Playing   Coombe
Place
Peneleway   Cowlands
Trelissick
Trevilla   Copeland
China
Feock   Towan
Nurseries
Camellia
Restronguet
Point   St. Just in
Roseland
Mylor
Churchtown   St. Just
Pool
Cross
Tregassic
ushing
St.
Mawes   Gerrans   Portscatho
Pencabe
Percuil
St. Anthony-
in-Roseland   Greeb Point
FALMOUTH
St. Mawes
Docks   Towan Beach
Falmouth
Docks   St. Anthony   Bohortha
Porthbeor
Beach
Porthmellin
Head
FALMOUTH   St.Anthony   Zone Point
Head
FALMOUTH
BAY

Cove

kerris Point
ow
encra head
houstock
t's Quoits
Manacle Point
The Manacles

d Point
Beach

Ruan
Lanihorne
Lamorran
Treworga
80
Philleigh   Ruan High
Lanes
Treworthal   Melinsey
Mill
Treworlas   Veryan
Treluggan   Carne
Carne
Trewithian   Beacon   Carne
Trewithian   Nare
Porthbean Beach   Head
Rosevine   Gull Rock
Porthcurnick Beach   Outer Stone
GERRANS
BAY
Liberick Cove

Veryan
Green   Hartriza Point
Veryan   Portloe
Manare Point
VERYAN
BAY

Polgrain   Rescassa
St. Michael
Penvose   Caerhays   Caerhays
Treveor
Portholland   Tregavarras
Perbargus   Boswi
Point   Greeb
Point
Round Houses   Greeb
Veryan   Point
Gell Point
High Point
Lizard Pool

Railways   Polkirt Beach
Gorran Tregerrick   Portmellon
High
Lanes   Chapel Point
NT   Colona Beach
Gorran   Pabyer Point
Churchtown   Great Perhaver
Beach
Gorran Haven

r Vault Beach   040

Penveor Point
NT

DODMAN POINT

9

1

2

3

30

20

10

12

C   D

C   D

90   200

10

A

B

70

40

¹50

1

60

2

⁰50

6

7

3

40

40

Godrevy Island
Godrevy Point
Nav

Porthmeor Beach

ST. IVES BAY
The Island or St. Ives Head   Peter's Point

Carn Naun   Pen Enys   Hor
Point   Point   Point
The
Carracks
Mussel Point
Zennor
Wayside
Folk
Gurnard's
Head
NT   Trereen Dinas
Bosigran
Castle   Porthmeor
Porthmeor Point
Treen
Three
Stone   The   Greeb
Oat   Mozens   Point
Portheras Co
Pendeen Watch

Zennor
B3306   247
Sperris Quoit
Zennor
Quoit   NT
Carn Galver Mine
Engine Houses

SWC Path   NT
NT   NT
Hellesveor
A

NT
Towednack

St. Ives
St Ives
Penbeagle
Halsetown
Bussow
Res
Knill's

LADY
DOWNS

Cripplesease

Porthminster
Point
Carbis
Bay   Porth Kidney
Sands

Bowl
Rock   Lelant
Merlins
Magic
Land
Trencrom Hill

Lelant
B   Lelant
The
Towans

Phillack
Copperhouse
Hayle
The Dungeons
Paradise Park

B3301

A30 p22 A1 A382 @ 17:00
A30 p20 B2a 16:30 (Launceston)
A30 — C1 @ 16:04
16:00 BUGLE
15:30 Heligan

Trago Mills · Teigngrace
Orchid Paradise
Kingsteignton · Bishopsteignton
Palace
Rural Life
Sprey Point
Teignmouth
Teignmouth
Shaldon
Grand Pier
South Knighton · Mile End
Highweek
Ringmore
Combeinteignhead
Wildlife Trust · Labrador Bay

NEWTON ABBOT
West Ogwell · Bradley
East Ogwell · Decoy
Abbotskerswell
Middle Rocombe
Lower Gabwell
Higher Gabwell
Stokeinteignhead
Hedgehog Hospital
Denbury
Pleasant View Nursery
Two Mile Oak Cross
A380
Kingskerswell
Coffinswell · Daccombe
Maidencombe
BABBACOMBE BAY
Ipplepen
Dainton · North Whilborough
Combe Fishacre
Compton
Combe Pafford
Watcombe Head
Model Village
Bygones
Edginswell · Shiphay
Babbacombe
Oddicombe Cliff Railway
Anstey's Cove
Compton
Cockington Court
Chelston
Torre
Black Head
Kents Cavern
Cockington
Torquay
Marldon
Churscombe
Littlehempston · Afton
TORQUAY
Berry Pomeroy
Blagdon
Collaton St. Mary
PAIGNTON
Paignton
Goodrington
Goodrington Sands
Saltern Cove
TOR BAY
otnes
True Street
Longcombe
A385
Aish
Yalberton
Goodrington
Elberry Cove
Churston Cove
Berry Head
Stoke Gabriel
Waddeton
Galmpton
Churston Ferrers
Brixham
BERRY HEAD
Ashprington
Priory Gatehouse
Cornworthy
East Cornworthy
Dittisham
Paignton & Dartmouth Steam Railway
Hillhead
St. Mary's Bay
Sharkham Point
Prehistoric Hill Settlement
Capton
Man Sands
NT
Long Sands
Scabbacombe Head
Coleton Fishacre
DARTMOUTH
Kingston
Hillfield · Norton
A3122
Kingswear
NT
Ivy Cove
Puccombe Cove
Bowden
Castle
Dartmouth
Inner Froward Point
Combe Point
Stoke Fleming
Blackpool
Matthew's Point
Leonard's Cove
Merrifield · Strete
Forest Cove
A379
Pilchard Cove
Strete Gate
Slapton
Normandy Landings Obelisk
START BAY
Slapton Ley
Sherman Tank
Torcross
Beesands
Tinsey Head

Hallsands
Nestley Point
START POINT

90   00

1
2
3

70
60
50
40

❶

❷

❸

The Mouls
Rumps NT *The Rumps*
Point NT
Newland ⌀
Pentire Point SWC
Doyden Castle
Port Quin Bay NT
NT Com Head
Port Quin
Longcross Victorian
Trelights

New Polzeath
Padstow Bay
Hayle Bay ℹ
Pentireglaze
Porteath Bee Centre
B331
Polzeath

Stepper Point
NT *Daymer Bay*
Trebetherick
Trevanger
18
St. Minver

Butter Hole
Gunver Head
Lifeboat Station
Pityme
Tredrizzick
B3314

Gulland Rock
Cat's Cove
Lifeboat Station
Polventon or Mother Ivey's Bay
Harlyn Bay
SWC
Crugmeer
Lifeboat Station
SWC Path
Rock
Splatt
Penmayne
Stoptide

TREVOSE HEAD
Dinas Head
Booby's Bay
Harlyn
Higher Harlyn
Trevone
Treator
Windmill
Padstow
Dinas
RIVER
Cant Hill
75
Lower Amb

Constantine Bay
18
Tregonce
Cant Cove
CAMEL Trewoman

Treyarnon Point
Treyarnon
Towan
St. Merryn
B3276
A389
Camel Trail
Tregunna
Trevanson

Fox Cove
Shop
Little Petherick
Edmonton
St. Breock
Lower Amb

Porthcothan Bay
NT
St. Merryn
Trevance
Whitecross

Porthcothan
Old Macdonald's Farm
Trenouth Rare Breeds Centre
St. Issey
Mellingey Mill
Trenance
Ryl. Cornwall Showground
Tre

NT
High Cove
Park Head
Treburrick
Penrose
Tamarisk
Rumford
Tredinnick

Bedruthan Steps
St. Ervan
Ⓐ
B3276
12
Trelow
St. Jidgey
A39
Pawton Quoit
Ⓑ
ST. BREOCK DOWNS
Stone
Monolith

High Cove
Trenance Point
St. Eval
Trevilledor
Shires
TRELOW DOWNS
ROSENANNON DOWNS
Nine Maidens Stone Row

Trenance
18
Lower Lanherne
DENZELL DOWNS
Winnard's

Berry's Point
Beacon Cove
Gluvian
Japanese
Cornish Birds

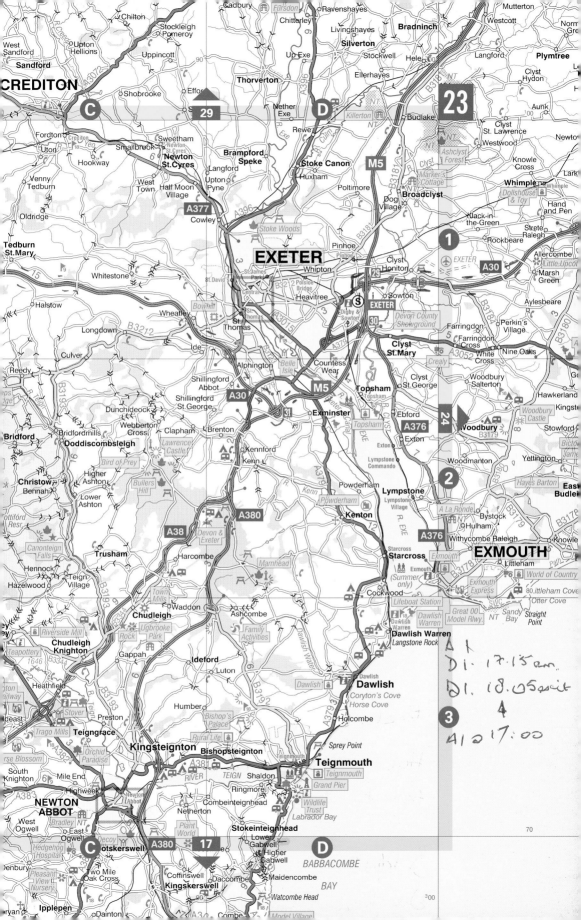

Exeter Services: 18:05.

Honiton A35.   18:24.

Axminster A35   18:38

Bridport   19:00

Dorchester   19:12   Poole   19:

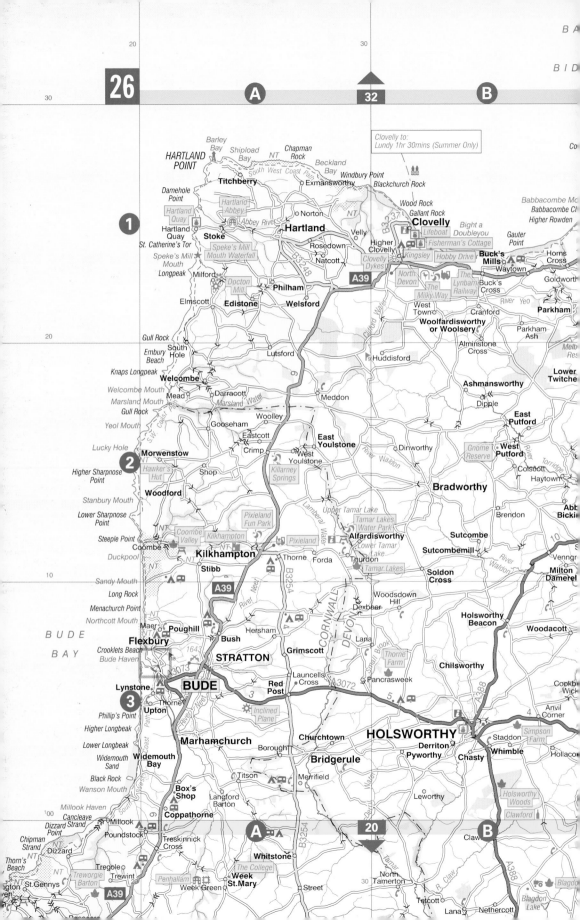

20   30

30

HARTLAND POINT
Barley Bay
Shipload Bay
NT
Chapman Rock
Beckland Bay
Windbury Point
Blackchurch Rock

Clovelly to:
Lundy 1hr 30mins (Summer Only)

Co

Titchberry
Exmansworthy
Wood Rock
Gallant Rock
Higher Rowden

Damehole Point
Hartland Abbey
Abbey River
NT
Clovelly
Lifeboat
Fisherman's Cottage
Bight a Doubleyou
Gauter Point

Babbacombe Mc
Babbacombe Cl

1
Hartland Quay
Hartland Quay
Abbey River
NT
Velly
Higher Clovelly
Kingsley
Hobby Drive
Buck's Mills
Horns Cross

Stoke
o Norton
Hartland
Rosedown
Clovelly Dykes
North Devon
The Lynbarn Railway
Waytown
Goldworth

St. Catherine's Tor
Speke's Mill Mouth Waterfall
Natcott
B3248
B3237
The Milky Way
Buck's Cross
Parkham

Speke's Mill Mouth
Longpeak
Milford
Philham
A39
West Town
Woolfardisworthy or Woolsery
Cranford
River Yeo

Elmscott
Docton Mill
Edistone
Welsford
Clovelly Water
Alminstone Cross
Parkham Ash

Gull Rock
South Hole
Lutsford
Huddisford
Lower Twitche

Embury Beach
Knaps Longpeak
Welcombe
Darracott
Meddon
Ashmansworthy
Dipple
Melb Res

Welcombe Mouth
Marsland Mouth
Mead
Marsland Water
Woolley
East Putford

Gull Rock
Yeol Mouth
Gooseham
Eastcott
East Youlstone
Dinworthy
West Putford

Lucky Hole
Morwenstow
Hawker's Hut
Crimp
West Youlstone
River Waldon
Colscott
Haytown
Torridge

Higher Sharpnose Point
Shop
Killarney Springs
Bradworthy

Woodford
Upper Tamar Lake
Lamberal Water
Brendon
Abb Bicki

Stanbury Mouth
Tamar Lakes Water Park
Lower Tamar Lake
Sutcombe

Lower Sharpnose Point
NT
Pixieland Fun Park
Pixieland
Thurdon
Tamar Lakes
Sutcombemill
River Waldon
Venngr

Steeple Point
Coombe Valley
Kilkhampton
Thorne
Forda
Alfardisworthy
Soldon Cross
Milton Damerel

Duckpool
NT
Coombe
Stibb
B3254
Woodsdown Hill
10

Sandy Mouth
NT
A39
River Neet
Dexbeer
Holsworthy Beacon
Woodacott

Long Rock
Menachurch Point
Northcott Mouth
NT
Hersham
Lana
Thorne Farm
Chilsworthy

BUDE BAY
Maer
Poughill
Bush
Grimscott
CORNWALL
DEVON
Small Brook

Crooklets Beach
Bude Haven
1643
STRATTON
Launcells Cross
Pancrasweek
A388

BUDE
Red Post
A3072
Churchtown
HOLSWORTHY
Derriton
Pyworthy
Staddon
Simpson Farm
Hollacc

Lynstone
Thorne
A3073
Bridgerule
Chasty
Whimble

3
Upton
Inclined Plane
Borough
Titson
Merrifield
Leworthy
Holsworthy Woods
Clawford

Phillip's Point
Higher Longbeak
Marhamchurch
Water
R. Claw

Lower Longbeak
Widemouth Sand
Widemouth Bay
Langford Barton
Box's Shop

Black Rock
Wanson Mouth
Coppathorne

Millook Haven
Cancleave
Dizzard Point
Millook
Poundstock
Treskinnick Cross
B3254
Whitstone
Claw

Chipman Strand
Dizzard
NT
Tregole Cross
Trewint
The College
Penhallam
Week St.Mary
North Tamerton
Telcott
Lana
Nethercott
Blagdon Lake
Blagdo

Thorn's Beach
Treworgie Barton
A39
Week Green
Street
30
Blagd

St. Gennys
A388
A39

BA
BID
BI

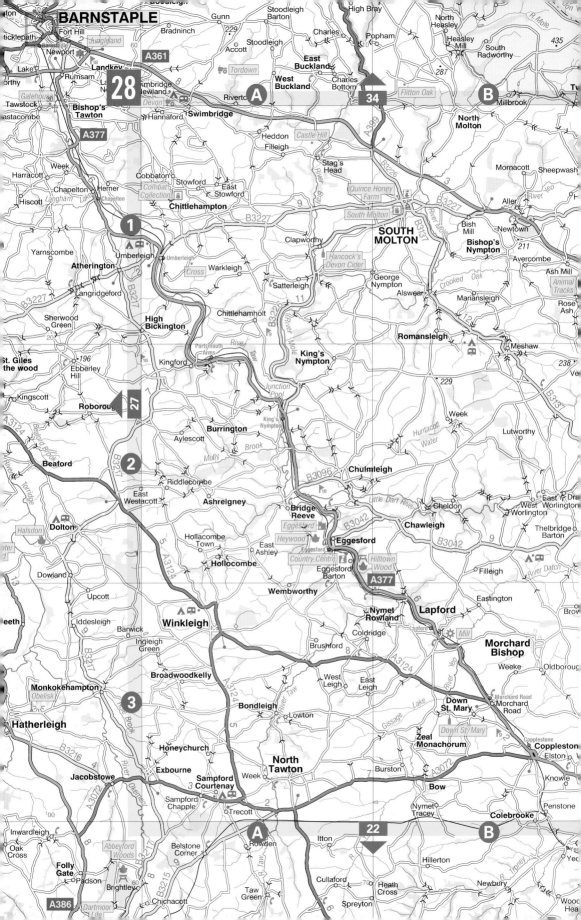

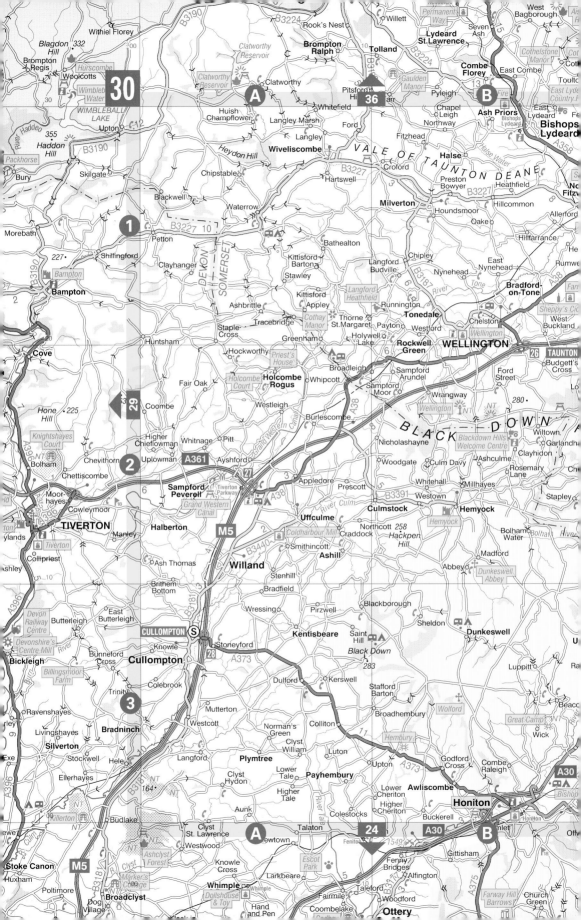

1

LUNDY

Lundy lies in the Bristol Channel 12 miles north west of Hartland Point. 3 miles long by between 0.25 and 0.75 miles wide and rising to over 130 m (427 ft), the island is almost completely made of light coloured granite covered in grass and heather. The west and south coasts are the finest with tall cliffs providing tremendous views over the 4,000 miles of the Atlantic, whilst the east and north coasts give views to the Devon coast and South Wales. The sea around Lundy is a designated Marine Nature Reserve noted for seals and famous for puffins.

Lundy was held by the piratical de Marisco family in the 13th century and later by the Royalists in the Civil War, the present castle being rebuilt during this time. There are three lighthouses, the Old Light of 1820 on Beacon Hill (the highest point of the island), designed by the architect of Dartmoor prison, was often obscured by mist and was replaced by the North and South Lights in 1897, both currently in use. Also of note are the Devil's Slide, a spectacular granite slab sloping into the sea on the west coast and the Devil's Limekiln, a deep hole at Shutter Point.

Lundy is owned by the National Trust but administered by the Landmark Trust who acquired the island in 1969. It has around twenty residents, no cars, a church, tavern and shop. The MS Oldenburg sails to the island from Bideford (2.25 hours) all year, and Ilfracombe (2.25 hours) and Clovelly (1.5 hours, less frequently) between April and October. Landing is by launch to the beach. Day trips, camping and longer stays in self catering accommodation are possible.

2

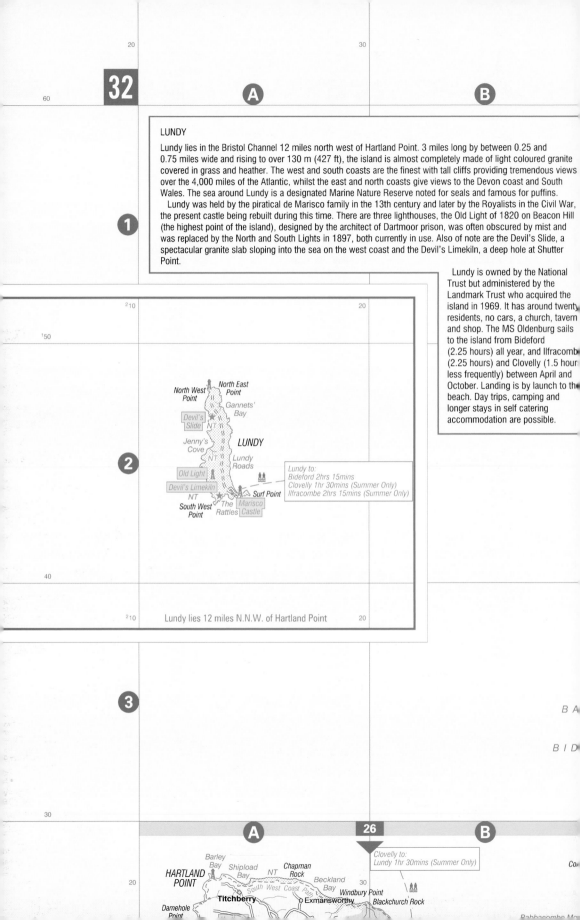

North West Point
North East Point
Gannets' Bay
Devil's Slide   NT
Jenny's Cove
NT
Old Light
Devil's Limekiln
NT
South West Point
The Rattles
LUNDY
Lundy Roads
Surf Point
Marisco Castle

Lundy to:
Bideford 2hrs 15mins
Clovelly 1hr 30mins (Summer Only)
Ilfracombe 2hrs 15mins (Summer Only)

Lundy lies 12 miles N.N.W. of Hartland Point

²10   20
¹50
40
²10   20

3

B A

B I D

Clovelly to:
Lundy 1hr 30mins (Summer Only)

HARTLAND POINT
Barley Bay
Shipload Bay   NT
Chapman Rock
Beckland Bay
Windbury Point
Blackchurch Rock
South West Coast Path
Titchberry
○ Exmansworthy
Damehole Point

Co

30

20

60   70

A   **B**

60

1

150

Foreland
Point

Lynmouth Bay   Cliffs   Countisbury
Cove

Highveer   Martinhoe   Lee Bay   **LYNTON**   Kipscombe Hill
Point   Beacon   342
Roman   Woody   Watersmeet   **Lynmouth**   Countisbury   A39
Fortlet   Bay   West Lyn   Lyn River

The Mare   Elwill   Heddon's   Woody Bay   Lynbridge   Wilsham   Leeford
& Colt   Bay   Cleave & Mouth   TOLL

Village Widmouth   Combe   Hangman   Blackstone   Heddon   Martinhoe   Dean   West Lyn   Rockford   Brendon
Point   Martin   Head   Point   Point   Valley   Trentishoe

Widmouth   Bay   Little   Holdstone Down   Cherrybridge   **Barbrook**   Tippacott   Malmsm
Hill   Hangman   349   NT   Kemacott   Martinhoe   East   Bridge Ball   Cheriton
Mill   Goosewell   Watermouth   309   Common   Cross   Ilkerton

Hagginton   Castle   Heale   West   Shilstone Hill
Combe   Killington   Ilkerton   Furzehill   405
Berrynarbor   Martin   Bodley   Shallowford
Pack O'   Dean   **Parracombe**   Churchtown   Brendon
Cards Inn   Holwell Castle   Common
Manor   **2**   Combe   **E X M O O R**

Henstridge   Martin   269   7   A399   Kentisbury   Chapman   Hoar Oak Tree   R.H. Maclaren
A3123   Berry Down   Barrows   480   Longstone
Cross   Kentisbury   337   **Blackmoor**   **F O R E S**
Ford   **Gate**   Pinkworthy   River Exe
Patchole   Wistlandpound   Pond   The Chains
Bittadon   Indicott   East   Reservoir   **E**
Down   Exmoor   B3358
Clifton   Arlington   475   **Challacombe**
258   Churchill   Beccott   Barton   Sloley Stone   River Barle   C
Arlington   Town   Shoulsbury   **Simonsbath**
ddle   Milltown   Arlington   Knightacott   Castle   Setta Barrow   Fortescue
wood   Court   Four   **EXM**
Higher   261   Cross   Western Common   Kingsford
Muddiford   Loxhore   Way   Exmoor Steam   493   Gate
wood   Muddiford   Leworthy   Railway   Five Barrows   Kinsford Water
Guineaford   **Shirwell**   Lower   **Bratton**   Lydcott   North   R. Mole
Prixford   Loxhore   **Fleming**   10   Radworthy   435
Hakeford   Brayfordhill   Holewater   North   South
A39   Stoke   **Brayford**   Heasley   Radworthy
Bradford   **3**   Northleigh   Rivers   High Bray   Heasley
Snapper   **Goodleigh**   Mill
ton   Gunn   Stoodleigh   Charles   287
BARNSTAPLE   Bradninch   229   Barton   Popham
Fort Hill   Jungleland   Accott   Stoodleigh   Charles
ticklepath   Newport   **East**   Bottom   **North**
Lake   A361   **Buckland**   **Molton**
rthy   **Landkey**   Landkey   Tordown   **West**   Flitton Oak
Rumsam   Newland   Swimbridge   **Buckland**   Millbrook
Gatehouse   Newland   Riverton   Charles   B3226
astacombe   North Devon   **28**
Tawstock   **Bishop's**   **Swimbridge**   **A**
orthy   **Tawton**   Hannaford
A377   Heddon   Castle Hill
Filleigh   Stag's   Mornacott   Sheepwash
Week   Head   B3226
Harracott   Cobbaton   Stowford   Quince Honey   Aller
Chapelton   Herner   Combat   East   Farm
Langham   Chapelton   Collection   Stowford

TOWN PLANS

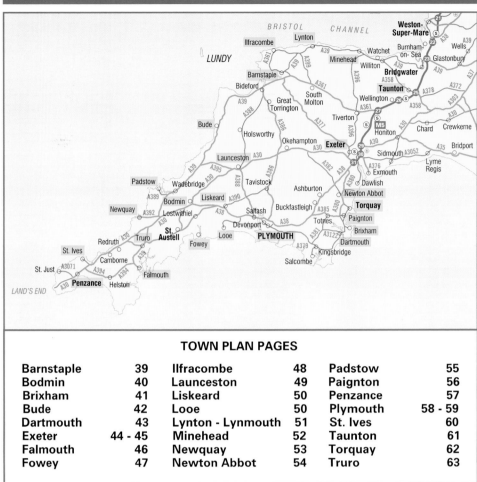

TOWN PLAN PAGES

TOWN PLAN ONLY SYMBOLS

SEE PAGE 5 FOR COMPLETE MAP AND TOURIST REFERENCES

RESTRICTED ACCESS		CAR PARK (selected)	P
PEDESTRIAN ROAD		CHURCH	†
MAIN FOOTPATH			
ONE WAY STREET		HOSPITAL	H
		MARKET	
RAILTRACK STATION		POLICE STATION	▲
HERITAGE, MINIATURE RAILWAY STATION		POST OFFICE	★
CITY WALL		SHOPMOBILITY	
BUS STATION		TOILET	▽

1: 15,840	SCALE	4 Inches (10 cm) to 1 Mile (1.584 Km)

0   ¼   ½   ¾   1 Mile

0   250m   500m   750m   1 Kilometre

Barnstaple is a market town and former port situated on the tidal River Taw where it is crossed by the widened 13th century sixteen arch Long Bridge. The town traded in Barum ware pottery and this is still made at Brannams Pottery (on Roundswell Industrial Estate to the south west). There is a Pannier Market in the large Market House on Butchers Row and on Paternoster Row nearby is St Anne's Chapel, an early chantry chapel once used as a grammar school. A pleasant riverside walk runs along the quay, off The Strand, leading to Queen Anne's Walk, a colonnaded arcade of 1796 with a statue of Queen Anne.

PLACES OF INTEREST
Tourist Information Centre (All year) - 36 Boutport Street. Tel: 01271 375000
◆ BARNSTAPLE CASTLE- Mound & traces of a moat of the former Norman castle. Tuly Street. ◆ BARNSTAPLE HERITAGE CENTRE - Displays on history of Barnstaple. Queen Anne's Walk, The Strand. ◆ NORTH DEVON, THE MUSEUM OF (MUSEUM ON THE SQUARE) - Pottery industry, Royal North Devon Yeomanry, Tarka Centre with natural history of otters. North Devon Athenaeum, The Square. ◆ TARKA TRAIL - 180 mile footpath. 29.5 miles from Braunton through Barnstaple & Bideford to Meeth are a cycleway on the former Southern Railway line. ◆ TAW TORRIDGE COUNTRY PARK - 8.5 mile linear country park between Barnstaple & Bideford on former Southern Railway line. Part of the Tarka Trail (see above) & the South West Coast Path.

ENTERTAINMENT
◆ Cinemas - Boutport Street.
◆ Theatres - Queens Theatre, Boutport Street.

SPORT & LEISURE
◆ Parks & Gardens - Castle Mound, Tuly Street. Pilton Park, Pilton Causeway. Rock Park, New Road.
◆ Sports Centres - North Devon Leisure Centre, Seven Brethren Bank, Sticklepath. Park School Community Sports Hall, Park Lane (SE Barnstaple).
◆ Swimming Pools - North Devon Leisure Centre (as above).
◆ Ten-Pin Bowling - Lets Go Superbowl, Braunton Road.

Hartland Point

Clovelly

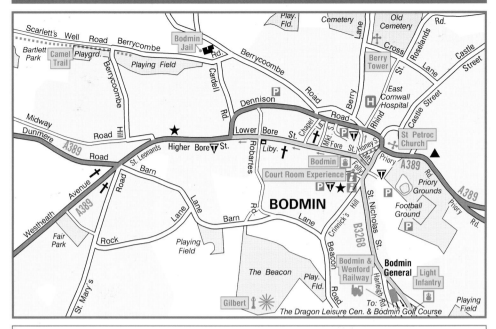

Bodmin, situated on a hillside site, is the former county town of Cornwall. The town had an important priory until the Dissolution. Of note are the neo-classical granite Shire Hall (the former County Assize Court building of 1838 on Mount Folly last used in 1988 - see below), the county prison and St Petroc's Church (see below). The Beacon has panoramic views.

PLACES OF INTEREST

Tourist Information Centre (All year)- The Shire Hall, Mount Folly. Tel: 01208 76616

◆ BERRY TOWER - Remains of tower of St Annes Priory. Old Cemetery, Berry Lane. ◆ BODMIN & WENFORD RAILWAY - 6 mile standard gauge steam railway. Stations at Bodmin General, Colesloggett Halt (for Cardinham Woods), Bodmin Parkway (main line) & Boscarne Junction (for Camel Trail). Bodmin General Station, Lostwithiel Road. ◆ BODMIN JAIL - Former county prison dating back to 1776. Exhibition with recreated displays in dungeons & cells. Berrycombe Road. ◆ BODMIN MUSEUM - History of Bodmin up to the end of WWII. Costumes, domestic and farming artifacts. Mount Folly. ◆ CAMEL TRAIL - Popular 17 mile cycleway & footpath on former LSWR railway line linking Padstow, Wadebridge & Bodmin, continuing to Poley's Bridge nr. Wenfordbridge. ◆ DUKE OF CORNWALL'S LIGHT INFANTRY MUSEUM - Regimental history, military artefacts, uniforms & medals. The Keep, Victoria Barracks, Plas Newydd Avenue. ◆ GILBERT MONUMENT - 44 m (144 ft) high granite obelisk in memory of Sir Walter Raleigh Gilbert. The Beacon. ◆ ST PETROC CHURCH - Cornwall's largest church containing 12th century reliquary of St Petroc. Priory Road. ◆ SHIRE HALL COURT ROOM EXPERIENCE - Recreation of 19th century trial of Charlotte Dymond, found murdered on Rough Tor in 1844, in original court building. Holding cells. The Shire Hall, Mount Folly. ◆ TOWN & COUNTRYSIDE CENTRE - History, wildlife, information on Camel trail, activities, places to see in Bodmin, on Bodmin Moor & in the surrounding area. The Shire Hall, Mount Folly.

SPORT & LEISURE

◆ Parks & Gardens - Fair Park, Westheath Avenue. Priory Ground, Priory Road. The Beacon, Beacon Rd.
◆ Sports Centres - The Dragon Leisure Centre, Lostwithiel Road (S of Bodmin General Station).
◆ Swimming Pools - The Dragon Leisure Centre (as above).

Cornish Countryside

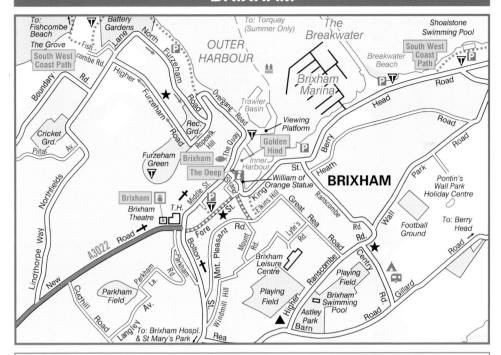

Brixham, a popular small fishing port with narrow streets, was described in 1850 as 'the largest fishery in England' and it is still an important trawler port with a busy fish market. The half mile long breakwater protects the outer harbour and Brixham Marina whilst a viewing platform on the New Pier (built in 1803/4), accessible to the public, overlooks the Trawler Basin. A statue on the Strand commemorates William of Orange's landing in Brixham in 1688 and preserved WWII gun battery emplacements can be seen in Battery Gardens.

PLACES OF INTEREST
Tourist Information Centre (All year)- The Old Market House, The Quay. Tel: 01803 852861
◆ BRIXHAM AQUARIUM - Marine life including sharks, octopi & eels. 12 The Quay. ◆ BRIXHAM MUSEUM - Local & maritime history including shipbuilding, smuggling, lifeboats, the coastguard, trawler models, pictures & costume. Bolton Cross, New Road. ◆ GOLDEN HIND, THE - Replica of Sir Francis Drake's ship on which he sailed around the world in 1577-80. Displays on life at sea. The Quay.
◆ THE DEEP - History, fables & monsters of the ocean. Re-creations of sea cave, trawler, sunken pirate ship featuring whales, mermaids & folklore. The Old Market House, The Quay.

ENTERTAINMENT
◆ Theatres - Brixham Theatre, New Road.

SPORT & LEISURE
◆ Parks & Gardens - Astley Park, Higher Ranscombe Road.
Battery Gardens, North Furzeham Road.
Furzeham Green, Higher Furzeham Road.
Parkham Field, Parkham Lane.
St Mary's Park, Upton Manor Road (S Brixham).
◆ Sports Centres - Brixham Leisure Centre, Lyte's Road.
◆ Swimming Pools - Brixham Swimming Pool, Higher Ranscombe Road. Shoalstone Swimming Pool, Berry Head Road.

Brixham

BUDE

Bude grew up as an agricultural trading port, serving the surrounding remote rural area, to which it was linked by the 35 mile long Bude Canal built in the 1820s. Known for its inclined planes instead of locks, the 2 miles to Helebridge survive with pleasant towpath walks. Bude later became a Victorian & Edwardian resort and it remains a popular family seaside destination. Crooklets Beach is used for surfing. The Castle (now council offices) was built in 1850 by Sir Goldsworthy Gurney, best known for his invention of incandescent lighting and the steam powered road coach.

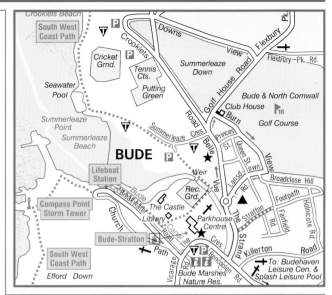

PLACES OF INTEREST

Tourist Information Centre
(All year)- Bude Visitor Centre,
The Crescent car park.
Tel: 01288 354240 ◆ BUDE-STRATTON MUSEUM - Displays on the Bude Canal, railway & local shipwrecks. Audio-visual. Lower Wharf. ◆ BUDE VISITOR CENTRE - Information on the natural history of the Bude area. The Crescent car park. ◆ COMPASS POINT STORM TOWER - Eight sided storm tower marked with points of the compass. Compass Point, Efford Down. ◆ LIFEBOAT STATION - Established in 1837. Inflatable 'D' lifeboat. South Lock Pier, Breakwater Road.

SPORT & LEISURE

◆ Parks & Gardens - Summerleaze Down, Crooklets Road.
◆ Sports Centres - Budehaven Leisure Centre, Budehaven School, Stratton Road.
◆ Swimming Pools - Seawater Pool, Summerleaze Beach. Splash Leisure Pool, Stratton Road.

Coastline Cornwall

DARTMOUTH

Dartmouth is an historic port and holiday centre on the west side of the beautiful land-locked estuary of the River Dart. Once important for the export of cloth and for trade with Newfoundland, the town is characterized by narrow streets, alleyways and long flights of steps such as Horn Hill and Browns Hill (once the main packhorse route). The South Embankment quay is ideal for harbour watching and from here the foot ferry crosses to Kingswear and popular river cruises leave for Totnes, 10 miles upstream, and trips past Dartmouth Castle downstream. Buildings of note include The Butterwalk in Duke Street dating from 1635-40 with elaborately carved overhanging timbers, the colonnaded Old Market House (dating from the 1830s) in Market Square and the famous Britannia Royal Naval College of 1905.

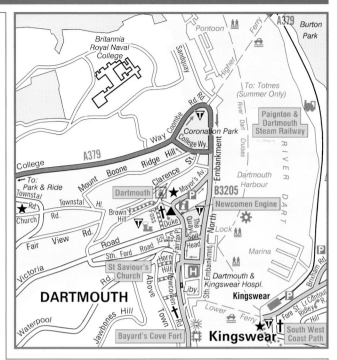

PLACES OF INTEREST

Tourist Information Centre (All year)- The Engine House, Mayor's Avenue. Tel: 01803 834224
◆ BAYARD'S COVE FORT (EH) - Small artillery fort of 1510 built to protect the harbour entrance. Riverfront, Southtown. ◆ DARTMOUTH MUSEUM - Maritime history, ship models, pictures and artifacts relating to Dartmouth & its estuary. The Butterwalk, Duke Street. ◆ NEWCOMEN MEMORIAL ENGINE - Engine of 1725, a memorial to Dartmouth born Thomas Newcomen, inventor of the atmospheric steam pumping engine. The Engine House, Royal Avenue Gardens, Mayor's Avenue. ◆ PAIGNTON & DARTMOUTH STEAM RAILWAY - 7 mile standard gauge steam railway using GWR engines. Stations at Kingswear, Churston, Goodrington, Paignton. Kingswear Station, Kingswear. ◆ ST SAVIOUR'S CHURCH - Noted for its 15th century ornate rood screen with painted panels of saints. Church Close.

SPORT & LEISURE

◆ Parks & Gardens - Coronation Park, North Embankment. Royal Avenue Gardens, Mayor's Avenue.

River Dart

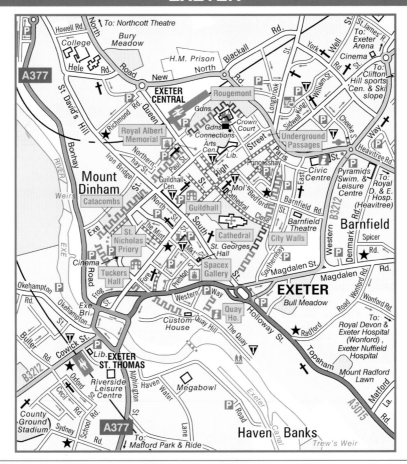

Exeter, a cathedral and university city, is the county 'town' of Devon and remains an historic city despite damage from wartime bombing raids in 1942. Of note are Fore Street, the cobbled Stepcote Hill (the only surviving medieval street in the city), Mol's Coffee House of 1596 in Cathedral Close and the Custom House of 1681 on the Quay. The city was once a major port exporting woollen cloth and is connected with the Exe estuary at Topsham by the 5 mile long Exeter Ship Canal, built in the 1560s, followed by a canalside walk. 'Exeter Historic Quayside' is now a popular waterside area with shops and restaurants.

Exeter Cathedral

Tudor Buildings, Exeter

Dart Valley

PLACES OF INTEREST

Tourist Information Centre (All year) - Civic Centre, Paris Street. Tel: 01392 265700

◆ CATACOMBS, THE - Underground catacombs of the citys 17th century old cemetery. Guided tours only (inquire at tourist information centre). Bartholomew Street East.

◆ EXETER CATHEDRAL - Symmetrical building with twin Norman towers, the peak of the Decorated Gothic style in England. Longest Gothic vaulted nave in the country. West front sculptures. Cathedral Close.

◆ EXETER CITY WALLS - Roman town wall of 200 AD rebuilt in medieval times (no gateways survive). Best sections off Southernhay West, Bartholomew Street East, Northernhay Street & Northernhay Gardens.

◆ EXETER GUILDHALL - One of the oldest municipal buildings to survive in England still in use, dating from 1330 with a pillared facade of 1593. City's silver & regalia on display. High Street.

◆ EXETER ROUGEMONT CASTLE - Early Norman gatehouse & fragments of wall remain. Crown Court of 1774 & Rougemont Gardens now occupy most of the site. Castle Street.

◆ EXETER UNDERGROUND PASSAGES - Medieval underground conduits built to supply fresh water to the city. Exhibition, audio-visual, guided tour. Britain's only subterranean waterways open to the public. Eastgate, off High Street (nr. Boots).

◆ QUAY HOUSE VISITOR CENTRE - History of the port of Exeter with models, paintings & artifacts. Audio-visual on story of Exeter from its Roman origins to the present day. 46 The Quay.

◆ ROYAL ALBERT MEMORIAL MUSEUM & ART GALLERY - Exeter silver, Devon archaeology & natural history, paintings by Devon artists, fine art, ceramics, glass. Queen Street.

◆ ST NICHOLAS PRIORY - Guest wing of an 11th century Benedictine priory with a Norman undercroft, kitchen & guest hall. The Mint, off Fore Street.

◆ SPACEX GALLERY - Changing contemporary art exhibitions. 45 Preston Street.

◆ TUCKERS HALL - Medieval guild hall of the Weavers, Fullers & Shearmen of the wool & cloth trade, with an arched braced roof of 1471. Fore Street.

ENTERTAINMENT

◆ Cinemas - Bartholomew Street West. Sidwell Street.

◆ Concerts- St Georges Hall, Market Street.

◆ Theatres- Barnfield Theatre, Barnfield Road. Exeter & Devon Arts Centre, Bradninch Place, Gandy Street. Northcott Theatre, University of Exeter Campus, Stocker Road, St David's (N of Exeter).

SPORT & LEISURE

◆ Parks & Gardens- Bull Meadow, Bull Meadow Road. Bury Meadow, North Road. Mount Radford Lawn, Topsham Road. Northernhay Gardens, Queen Street. Rougemont Gardens, Castle Street.

◆ Sports Centres - Clifton Hill Sports Centre, Clifton Hill (NE Exeter). County Ground Stadium, off Cowick Street. Exeter Arena Athletic Stadium, Summer Lane (NE Exeter). Pyramids Swimming & Leisure Centre, Heavitree Road Riverside Leisure Centre, The Plaza, Cowick Street. St James' Sports Centre, St James' High School, Summer Lane (NE Exeter). St Peter's Sports Centre, St Peter's High School, Quarry Lane (E Exeter). Wonford Sports Centre, Burnthouse Lane (SE Exeter).

◆ Ski Slope - Clifton Hill Sports Centre (as above).

◆ Swimming Pools - Northbrook Swimming Pool, Beacon Lane (NE Exeter). Pyramids Swimming & Leisure Centre (as above). Riverside Leisure Centre (as above).

◆ Ten Pin Bowling- Exeter Megabowl, Haven Banks Retail Park, Water Lane.

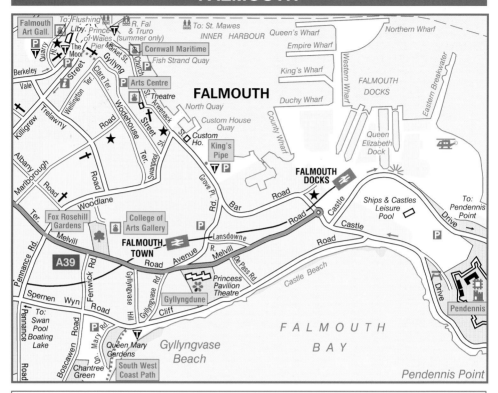

Falmouth Harbour and Carrick Roads form the largest natural haven in Britain. The port, developed in the 16th century by the Killigrew family, thrived by becoming a packet station for the Post Office between 1688 and 1852. It is now a major sailing centre with ship repair facilities centred on Falmouth Docks, best viewed from Castle Drive. Ferries to St Mawes, Flushing and along the River Fal to Truro leave from the Prince of Wales Pier. The town is noted for its gardens and parks with sub-tropical plants.

PLACES OF INTEREST

Tourist Information Centre (All year)- 28 Killigrew Street. Tel: 01326 312300
◆ CORNWALL MARITIME MUSEUM - Maritime history of Cornwall & mail carrying packet ships. Ship & port models. Bell's Court, Market Street.
◆ FALMOUTH ART GALLERY - Changing art exhibitions in late 19th century Passmore Edwards Library. Municipal Buildings, The Moor.
◆ FALMOUTH ARTS CENTRE - Changing fine art exhibitions in four galleries. 24 Church Street.
◆ FALMOUTH COLLEGE OF ARTS GALLERY - Students & visiting artists exhibitions. Falmouth College of Arts, Woodlane.
◆ FOX ROSEHILL GARDENS - 2 acre gardens containing exotic tree species including lemon, banana, eucalyptus & palms. Melvill Road.
◆ GYLLYNGDUNE GARDENS - Falmouth's finest formal gardens linked to seafront by a grotto walkway. Melvill Road.
◆ KING'S PIPE - Brick chimney once used to burn contraband tobacco. Arwenack Street.
◆ PENDENNIS CASTLE (EH) - Henry VIII castle with three storey circular keep & extensive outworks. Discovery Centre (Tudor gun-deck), WWII underground tunnels. Castle Drive.

ENTERTAINMENT

◆ Theatres - Falmouth Arts Centre (see above). Princess Pavilion Theatre, Melvill Road.

SPORT & LEISURE

◆ Parks & Gardens - Fox Rosehill Gardens (see above). Gyllyngdune Gardens (see above). Kimberley Park, Kimberley Park Road (W Falmouth). Queen Mary Gardens, Queen Mary Road. Swan Pool Boating Lake, Swanpool Road (SW Falmouth).
◆ Swimming Pools - Ships & Castles Leisure Pool, Castle Drive.

Fowey, one of the most important ports of medieval England, is situated on a deep water estuary used by bulk carriers for the export of china clay from the docks upstream. Justly famous for its beautiful harbour, with colourful yachts viewable from the Town Quay, the town has associations with novelist Daphne du Maurier who lived at Ferryside in Bodinnick and scholar and novelist Sir Arthur Quiller-Couch (known by the pseudonym 'Q') who lived at The Haven, Esplanade. The 15th century castellated mansion of Place is the home of the Treffry Family.

PLACES OF INTEREST

Tourist Information Centre (All year) - The Ticket Shop, 4 Custom House Hill.
Tel: 01726 833616

◆ DAPHNE DU MAURIER LITERARY CENTRE - Exhibition & audio-visual display reflecting the novelists life & works. 5 South Street.

◆ FOWEY AQUARIUM - Marine aquarium exhibiting species caught locally. Old Town Hall, Town Quay.

◆ FOWEY MUSEUM - History of port of Fowey, ship models, local interest. Old Town Hall, Town Quay.

◆ HALL WALK (NT) - 16th century walk from Bodinnick to Penleath Point, where King Charles I was fired upon in 1644. (see 'Q' Memorial' below) ◆ HEADLAND GARDEN - 1 1/4 ac. cliff garden. Plants & trees resistant to salt-laden gales. Sub-tropical plants. 3 Battery Lane, Polruan. ◆ OLD HOUSE OF FOYE - Reputed oldest house in Fowey, c1430. Old kitchen, beams etc. Fore Street. ◆ POLRUAN & FOWEY BLOCKHOUSES - Built in the late 15th century either side of the harbour, a chain boom was hung between the blockhouses to prevent the entry of enemy vessels. Polruan Blockhouse is best preserved. ◆ ST CATHERINE'S CASTLE (EH) - Small defensive Henry VIII coastal fort c1530. Above Readymoney Cove. ◆ SIR ARTHUR QUILLER-COUCH MEMORIAL (NT) - Monument & famous viewpoint over Fowey, estuary & Pont Pill creek. Hall Walk, Bodinnick.

SPORT & LEISURE

◆ Parks & Gardens - Squires Field, Park Road.

Fowey

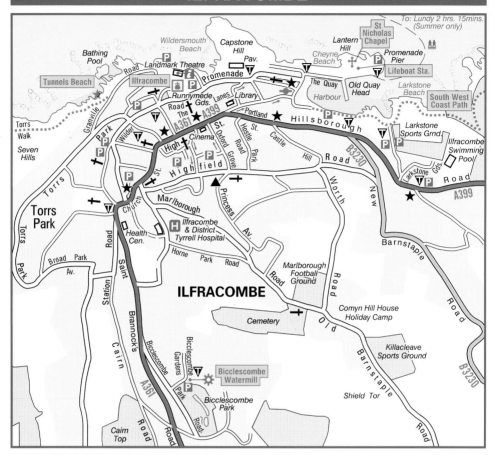

Ilfracombe, the picturesque town with its spectacular scenery and ancient harbour is North Devon's most popular seaside resort. The network of passages running from the High Street to the Sea Front known as 'The Lanes' enable the pedestrian to explore Ilfracombe along some of its oldest paths. A section has been developed into a sculpture trail with mosaics depicting various features characteristic of the town. The South West coastal path runs through Ilfracombe and the famous Torrs Walk heads out west to the village of Lee offering extensive views as you walk along the cliff top. In the summer months, the MS Oldenburg runs regular sailings to Lundy Island.

PLACES OF INTEREST
Tourist Information Centre (All year) - The Landmark Theatre, The Seafront. Tel: 01271 863001
◆ BICCLESCOMBE WATERMILL - Restored 18th century mill. Runs during the Summer for demonstration purposes only. Bicclescombe Park, Bicclescombe Gardens. ◆ ILFRACOMBE MUSEUM - Located in a building dating from 1885, this intriguing collection contains over 20,000 exhibits of natural history along with war memorabilia, paintings, photographs & Victoriana which reflect life of a bygone age. There is also a brass-rubbing centre. Runnymede Gardens, Wilder Road. ◆ LIFEBOAT STATION - Established 1828. Inflatable 'D' & Mersey Class lifeboats. Cove car park, The Quay. ◆ ST NICHOLAS CHAPEL - 14th century chapel has been used as a lighthouse to guide seafarers into the harbour since 1522. Small exhibition illustrating the history of the chapel & local area. Lantern Hill, The Quay.
◆ TUNNELS BEACH - Approximately 150 years ago, 4 tunnels were created by cutting through solid rock to provide access to this famous beach location. Granville Road.

ENTERTAINMENT
◆ Cinemas - 134 High Street. Landmark Theatre, The Promenade.
◆ Theatres - Landmark Theatre (see above).

SPORT & LEISURE
◆ Parks & Gardens - Bicclescombe Park, Bicclescombe Road. Runnymede Gardens, Wilder Road.
◆ Swimming Pools - Ilfracombe Swimming Pool, Hillsborough Road.

LAUNCESTON

Launceston, an ancient medieval hill top town, was the only walled town in Cornwall and until 1835 was the county's capital. Dunheved, the old town, is dominated by the castle and has many narrow twisting streets, of note being Castle Street with its brick Georgian houses. The town once had two railway stations at Newport served by two competing companies.

PLACES OF INTEREST

Tourist Information Centre (All year) - Market House Arcade, Market Street.
Tel: 01566 772321 / 772333
◆ LAUNCESTON CASTLE (EH) - Norman motte with shell keep & cylindrical tower providing commanding views. Castle Street. ◆ LAUNCESTON STEAM RAILWAY - 2 mile 2ft. gauge steam railway using Victorian locomotives on route of former North Cornwall line. Stations at Launceston, Hunts

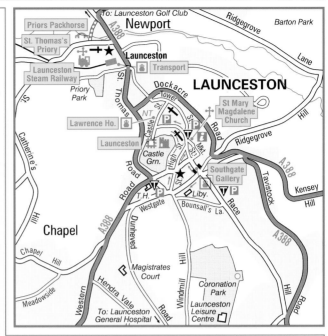

Crossing, Deer Park & Newmills (picnic site). Launceston Station, Newport Industrial Estate, St Thomas Road. ◆ LAUNCESTON STEAM RAILWAY TRANSPORT MUSEUM - Vintage cars, motorcycles, stationary steam engines. Launceston Steam Railway (see above).
◆ LAWRENCE HOUSE MUSEUM (NT) - Georgian house of 1753 housing museum of local history. Victorian dressing room & costumes. 9 Castle Street. ◆ PRIORS PACKHORSE BRIDGE - Ancient five arched packhorse bridge over River Kensey. Westbridge Road. ◆ ST MARY MAGDALENE CHURCH - Exterior adorned with decorative carvings (apart from tower) datings from early 16th century. Church Street.
◆ ST THOMAS'S PRIORY - Ruins of 12th century Augustinian Priory behind St Thomas's church. Riverside. ◆ SOUTHGATE GALLERY - Art gallery in room above the narrow arch of Southgate, a surviving part of the former 16th century town walls. Southgate Street.

SPORT & LEISURE

◆ Parks & Gardens - Castle Green, Castle Street. Coronation Park, Dunheved Road.
◆ Sports Centres - Launceston Leisure Centre, Coronation Park, Dunheved Road.
◆ Swimming Pools - Launceston Leisure Centre (as above)

Ilfracombe

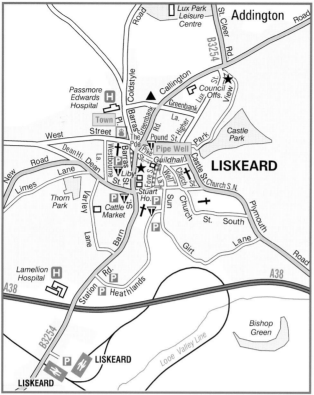

Liskeard, one of four former Stannary (or coinage) towns for the tin industry, is a busy hill top market town. The town has many fine Georgian buildings in the Parade, the 1850s Italian style Victorian Guildhall with tall clock tower in Pike Street and the late 19th century Passmore Edwards Library, together with Stuart House, in Barras Street. Castle Park is the former site of the castle and at 150 m (492 ft) provides good views. The Looe Valley Line is a scenic 8.5 mile branch railway line to Looe.

PLACES OF INTEREST
◆ LISKEARD TOWN MUSEUM- Local history of Liskeard. 5 West Street. ◆ PIPE WELL - Four spout well never known to dry up, also known as St Martins Well, on site of Market Hall. Well Lane.

SPORT & LEISURE
◆ Parks & Gardens - Castle Park, Castle Street. Thorn Park, Limes Lane.◆ Sports Centres - Lux Park Leisure Centre, Coldstyle Road. ◆ Swimming Pools - Lux Park Leisure Centre (as above).

Looe is a busy fishing port famous as a shark fishing centre. Situated on a narrow estuary at the confluence of the two Looe rivers it is divided into East Looe with its small narrow streets and West Looe, its quieter counterpart, linked together by a bridge built in 1855. A fish market is held on Buller Quay and the beach near the Banjo Pier is popular. The Looe Valley Line is a scenic 8.5 mile branch railway line to Liskeard.

PLACES OF INTEREST
Tourist Information Centre (Summer only) - The Guildhall, Fore Street, East Looe. Tel: 01503 262072
◆ LIFEBOAT STATION - Established in 1992. Inflatable 'D' lifeboat. Buller Quay, Buller Street, East Looe. ◆ LIVING FROM THE SEA AQUARIUM - Species caught around the Cornish coast. World of Sharks Exhibition. History of the Cornish fisherman. Buller Quay, East Looe. ◆ OLD GUILDHALL MUSEUM - 15th century guildhall. Displays on local history, fishing, boat building & smuggling. Exhibits include toys, model ships & the old cells. Higher Market Street, East Looe. ◆ SOUTH EAST CORNWALL DISCOVERY CENTRE - Visitor centre with displays on wildlife & heritage of SE Cornwall. Video & photographic exhibition. Millpool, West Looe.

ENTERTAINMENT
◆ Cinemas - Higher Market Street, East Looe.

SPORT & LEISURE
◆ Parks & Gardens - Hannafore Road, West Looe. West Looe Downs, West Road, West Looe.

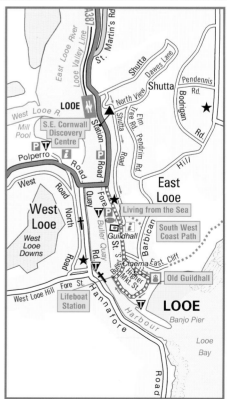

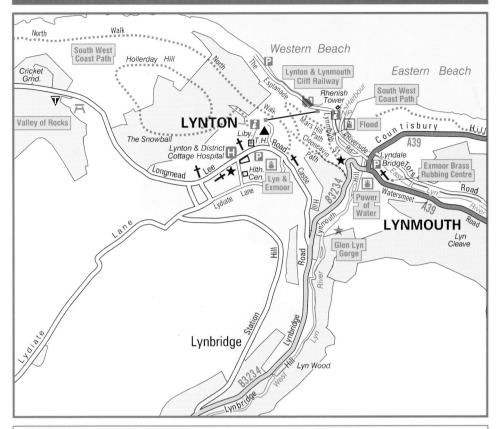

Separated vertically by 152 m (500 ft), the twin villages of Lynton and Lynmouth are linked by a unique water powered cliff railway. The vulnerability of Lynmouth's location lying on the shore where the valleys of the East and West Lyn converge made it the victim of the 1952 flood when 90 million gallons of water fell in a single night. The Rhenish Tower which was originally built in 1855 by Colonel Rawdon was rebuilt following its destruction in the disaster. Lynmouth was once famous for its large catches of herring and curing houses known as 'Red Herring Houses' lined both sides of the river. Lynton and Lynmouth developed rapidly as a tourist destination with its natural beauty and tranquility making it a favourable destination for the traveller. Today numerous walks exemplify the natural beauty of the area; paths over Hollerday Hill lead to the Valley of Rocks and Mars Hill is renowned for its thatched cottages.

PLACES OF INTEREST

Tourist Information Centre (All year) - Town Hall, Lee Road, Lynton. Tel: 01598 752225

◆ EXMOOR BRASS RUBBING CENTRE - Houses over 100 brass facsimiles dating from 1277. The collection which includes knights, clergy & animals is one of the largest available to the public. Woodside Craft Centre, Watersmeet Road, Lynmouth.

◆ GLEN LYN GORGE - Walks lead up through the woodland passing cascades & waterfalls to the ravine. Flood level marks from the 1952 catastrophe can be seen & England's largest privately owned hydro-electric station opened here in 1985. Watersmeet Road, Lynmouth.

◆ LYN & EXMOOR MUSEUM - Housed in a 17th century cottage the museum offers a comprehensive reflection of life in the area from the stone age to the modern day. St Vincent Cottage, Market Street, Lynton. ◆ LYNMOUTH FLOOD EXHIBITION - Exhibition recalls the devastation caused by the flood of 1952. Memorial Hall, Riverside Road, Lynmouth. ◆ LYNMOUTH VISITOR CENTRE (NP) - Displays recall the famous rescue of 1899 when the Lynmouth lifeboat was hauled 13 miles over land to launch at Porlock Weir. The Esplanade, Lynmouth. ◆ LYNTON & LYNMOUTH CLIFF RAILWAY - Officially opened in 1890, the railway is the last working water powered Victorian cliff railway in Europe. Rises 152 m (500 ft) over the 263 m (862 ft) of track from Lynmouth to Lynton. The Esplanade, Lynmouth & Lee Road, Lynton.

◆ POWER OF WATER EXHIBITION - Displays illustrate the various uses of water. Exhibition of steam engine models. Old Chapel, Glen Lyn Gorge, Watersmeet Road, Lynmouth.

◆ VALLEY OF ROCKS, THE - Famous dry valley thought to be a glacial meltwater channel formed during the Ice Age. Other formations include Castle Rock, Ragged Jack & Devil's Cheesewring. Lynton.

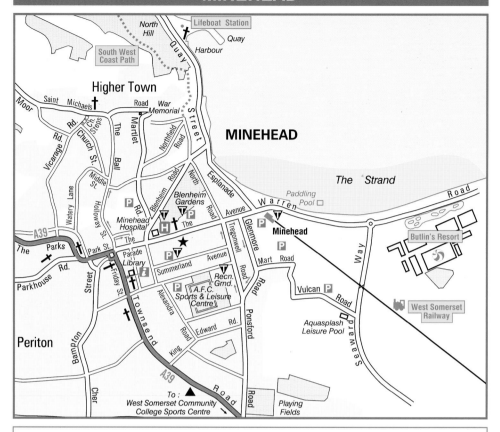

The popular holiday resort of Minehead lies on the north eastern edge of Exmoor between the National Park and the coast. The development of the town centred around the quay which offered safety and shelter on a coastal front that was both exposed and hazardous. The Higher Town retains much of its charm with thatched cottages and narrow alleyways, a favourite is Church Steps which leads up to the 14th century St Michael's Church on North Hill with spectacular views over the town. The old almhouses are on Market House Lane and nearby are the picturesque Blenheim Gardens. Minehead is the starting point of Britain's longest footpath, the 500 mile South West Coast Path.

PLACES OF INTEREST

Tourist Information Centre (All year) - 17 Friday Street. Tel: 01643 702624

◆ BUTLIN'S FAMILY ENTERTAINMENT RESORT - Large entertainment complex offering a diverse range of activities including sub-tropical waterworld with flume rides & rapids, funfair, leisure dome & boating lake. The Seafront, Warren Road.

◆ LIFEBOAT STATION - Established in 1901. Atlantic 75 class & Inflatable 'D' lifeboats. The Harbour.

◆ WEST SOMERSET RAILWAY - Steam trains run from Minehead to Bishop's Lydeard on the line that was closed by British Rail in 1971. The reopening of the line in 1976 created the longest independent railway in Britain. The Station, The Sea Front.

ENTERTAINMENT

◆ Cinemas - Butlin's Family Entertainment Resort (see above).

◆ Theatre - Regal Theatre, The Avenue.

SPORT & LEISURE

◆ Parks & Gardens - Blenheim Gardens, Blenheim Road.

◆ Sports Centres - West Somerset Community College Sports Centre, Bircham Road (SE Minehead).

◆ Swimming Pools - Aquasplash Leisure Pool, Seaward Way. Butlin's Somerwest World Holiday Centre (see above).

◆ Ten Pin Bowling - Butlin's Family Entertainment Resort (see above).

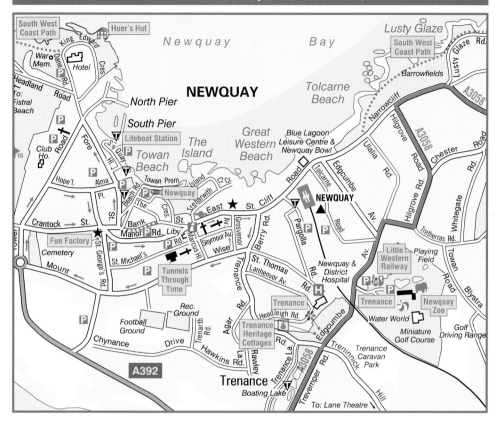

Newquay, Cornwall's favourite holiday resort, is famous for its Atlantic rollers, making it a centre for surfing, and for its expanses of sandy beaches of which west facing Fistral Beach (to the west of the town) is the largest and most popular. Once important as a fishing port, due largely to huge shoals of pilchards, and for the export of china clay, the town became a tourist destination with the coming of the railway in 1875.

PLACES OF INTEREST

Tourist Information Centre (All year) - Municipal Offices, Marcus Hill. Tel: 01637 871345
◆ FUN FACTORY - Indoor adventure play centre for the under 12s. 1 St Georges Road.
◆ HUER'S HUT - Small clifftop building from which the Huer watched for pilchard shoals. King Edward Crescent. ◆ LIFEBOAT STATION - Established in 1860. Atlantic 75 & Inflatable 'D' lifeboats. South Quay, Newquay Harbour. ◆ LITTLE WESTERN RAILWAY - 7.25" gauge circular miniature railway. Trenance Leisure Park, Edgcumbe Avenue. ◆ NEWQUAY SEA LIFE AQUARIUM - 70 species. Sharks, stingrays, seahorses. Lair of the Octopus. Underwater tunnel. Towan Promenade. ◆ NEWQUAY ZOO - 10 acres of lakeside gardens with over 300 animals. Tropical & Nocturnal Houses, Animal encounters, Dragon Maze. Trenance Leisure Park, Edgcumbe Avenue. ◆ TRENANCE HERITAGE COTTAGES - Displays of Cornish way of life in the 1900's. Trenance Gardens, Trenance Road.
◆ TRENANCE GARDENS - Outstanding municipal gardens, boating lake. Trenance Road.
◆ TRENANCE LEISURE PARK - 26 acre sport & leisure park. Edgcumbe Avenue.
◆ TUNNELS THROUGH TIME - Recreation of the stories & legends of Cornwall using life-size figures. St Michaels Road.

ENTERTAINMENT
◆ Theatres - Lane Theatre, Lane (SE of Newquay).

SPORT & LEISURE
◆ Parks & Gardens - Trenance Gardens (see above). Trenance Leisure Park (see above).
◆ Sports Centres - Newquay Sports Centre, Tretherras Road (E Newquay).
◆ Swimming Pools - Newquay Water World, Trenance Leisure Park. Splash City, Blue Lagoon Leisure Centre, Cliff Road.
◆ Ten-Pin Bowling - Newquay Bowl, Blue Lagoon Leisure Centre, Cliff Road.

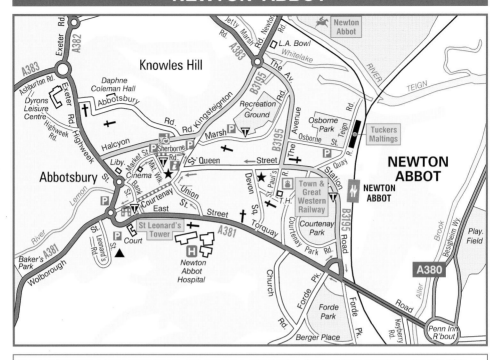

Newton Abbot is a busy market town and, since the arrival of the South Devon Railway in the mid 19th century, a railway town with typical railway terraces. It is situated at the head of the River Teign estuary where the Stover Canal brought down clay, and granite from quarries on Dartmoor served by the Haytor Granite Tramway, for export. The Templer Way follows much of the route.

PLACES OF INTEREST

Tourist Information Centre (All year) - 6 Bridge House, Courtenay Street. Tel: 01626 367494

◆ NEWTON ABBOT RACECOURSE - Between Newton Abbot & Kingsteignton. Newton Road.

◆ NEWTON ABBOT TOWN & GREAT WESTERN RAILWAY MUSEUM - History of town & its railway. Working signal box. GWR artifacts & photographs. 2a St Paul's Road.

◆ ST LEONARD'S TOWER - 14th century clock-tower (the remains of St Leonard's Church) where William III, Prince of Orange, was declared king in 1688. Courtenay Street.

◆ TUCKERS MALTINGS - Guided tours of traditional working malthouse where barley is turned into malt using original Victorian machinery. Teign Road, Osborne Park.

ENTERTAINMENT
◆ Cinemas - Market Street.

SPORT & LEISURE
◆ Parks & Gardens - Baker's Park, Wolborough Street. Courtenay Park, Courtenay Park Road. Forde Park, Forde Park. Osborne Park, Osborne Street.

◆ Sports Centres - Dyrons Leisure Centre, Wain Lane.

◆ Swimming Pools - Dyrons Leisure Centre (as above).

◆ Ten-Pin Bowling - L.A. Bowl, Kingsteignton Road.

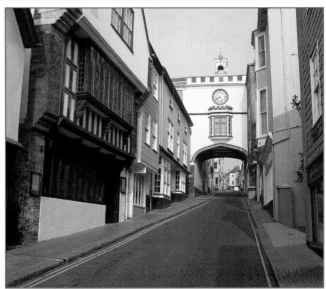

Fore Street, Totnes

Padstow is a popular resort on the River Camel Estuary. A fishing port with narrow winding streets converging on the picturesque and ancient harbour, the town was once the western outpost of the London & South Western Railway, closed in 1967 and now the Camel Trail. The pagan 'Obby 'Oss festival is held on May Day to celebrate the coming of Summer. There are no beaches in Padstow however a ferry leaves from the North Quay, or Lower Beach at low tide, to beaches at Rock across the estuary.

PLACES OF INTEREST

Tourist Information Centre (All year) - Red Brick Building, North Quay. Tel: 01841 533449

◆ CAMEL TRAIL - Popular 17 mile cycleway & footpath on former railway line starting at Padstow and linking to Wadebridge & Bodmin.

◆ PADSTOW MUSEUM - Local history. Displays on Padstow lifeboat, customs, railway. Ship paintings. Town Library, The Institute, Market Place.

◆ PRIDEAUX PLACE - Elizabethan mansion completed in 1592. Formal garden & landscaped deer park. Tregirls Lane.

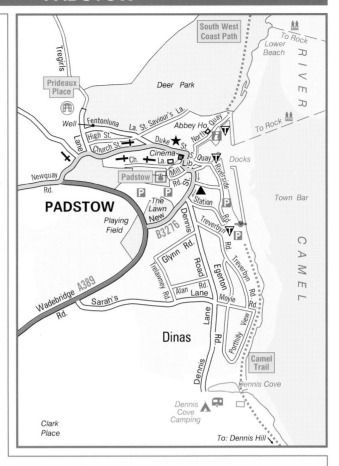

ENTERTAINMENT
◆ Cinemas- Lanadwell Street.

SPORT & LEISURE
◆ Parks & Gardens- The Lawn, New Street.

Padstow Harbour

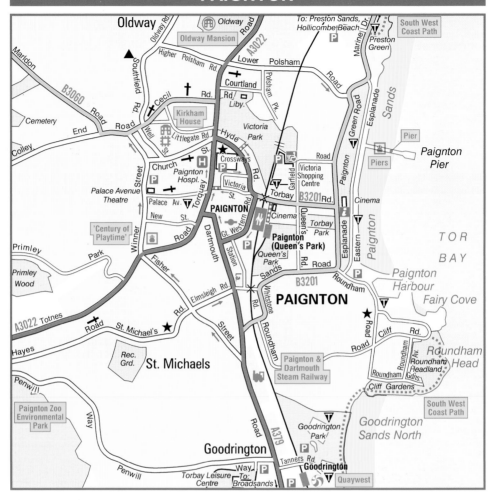

Paignton is a very popular family seaside resort which developed as a close neighbour of Torquay after the arrival of the railway in the mid 19th century. There are gardens, a pier, a long seafront (with the sandy beach of Paignton Sands adjacent to Paignton Green) and a small harbour at the end of the Esplanade. Other popular sandy beaches are Goodrington Sands, Broadsands to the south, and Preston Sands and Hollicombe Beach.

PLACES OF INTEREST

Tourist Information Centre (All year) - multiplex cinema, The Esplanade. Tel: 01803 558383
◆ 'CENTURY OF PLAYTIME'- DOLL & TOY MUSEUM - Old dolls & toys. 30 Winner Street.
◆ KIRKHAM HOUSE (EH) - 15th century stone merchant's town house. Old hall, furniture displays. Kirkham Street. ◆ OLDWAY MANSION - Begun by Isaac Singer (founder of the famous sewing machine company) in 1875 in the style of the Palace of Versailles with 17 acres of landscaped gardens. Torquay Road.
◆ PAIGNTON & DARTMOUTH STEAM RAILWAY - 7 mile standard gauge steam railway running along the scenic Torbay coast & Dart estuary to Kingswear. Stations also at Goodrington & Churston. Paignton (Queen's Park) Station, Torbay Road. ◆ PAIGNTON PIER & PIERS MUSEUM - Amusements, childrens rides, old slot machines. Paignton Sands. ◆ PAIGNTON ZOO ENVIROMENTAL PARK - 75 acres of gardens with lions, tigers, elephant & giraffe house, ape centre, baboon rock, aviary.- Totnes Road. ◆ QUAYWEST - Waterpark with 8 water flumes including the highest in England at 20 m (65 ft). Swimming pools, amusement rides. Goodrington Sands.

ENTERTAINMENT

◆ Cinemas - Esplanade Road. Torbay Road. Theatres- Palace Avenue Theatre, Palace Avenue.
SPORT & LEISURE
◆ Parks & Gardens - Goodrington Park, Tanners Rd. Oldway, Torquay Rd.Paignton Green, Eastern Esplanade. Preston Green, Marine Drive. Queen's Park, Queen's Road. Roundham Headland & Cliff Gardens, Roundham Gardens. Torbay Park, Esplanade Road. Victoria Park, Hyde Road. ◆ Sports Centres - Torbay Leisure Centre, Clennon Valley, Penwill Way. ◆ Swimming Pools - Quaywest (see above). Torbay Leisure Centre (as above).

Penzance, a port and resort characterized by its 19th century granite buildings, has developed as a market town for West Cornwall, its status being promoted by becoming the western terminus of the former Great Western Railway. Buildings of note include the imposing domed Market House (1838) at the top of Market Jew Street with the statue of Sir Humphry Davy (born 1778), inventor of the miner's safety lamp, below it and St John's Hall on Alverton Street, built in the 1860s, one of the largest granite buildings in Britain. There are two parks with sub-tropical plants off Morrab Road. Regular ferries leave Lighthouse Pier for St Mary's in the Isles of Scilly; helicopter flights leave from the heliport off the A30 to the east of the town.

PLACES OF INTEREST
Tourist Information Centre (All year) - Station Road. Tel: 01736 362207
◆ CORNWALL GEOLOGICAL MUSEUM - Cornish rocks, minerals & fossils. Mining & quarrying displays. St John's Hall, Alverton Street. ◆ EGYPTIAN HOUSE - Building with elaborate painted Eygptian style facade built in 1836. Chapel Street. ◆ NEWLYN ART GALLERY- Changing exhibitions of contemporary paintings & sculpture in Passmore Edwards building. Newlyn Green, New Road, Newlyn. ◆ PENLEE HOUSE GALLERY & MUSEUM - History of West Cornwall from stone age to present day. Largest art collection in West Cornwall dating from 1750 including artists of the famous Newlyn School. Morrab Road. ◆ PENZANCE MARITIME MUSEUM - Full size recreation of part of early 18th century warship. Treasure & artefacts recovered by diving expeditions. 19 Chapel Street. ◆ PILCHARD WORKS - Britain's last working salt pilchard factory. Factory visit to press room & heritage centre with photographs, paintings & artefacts. Tolcarne, The Coombe, Newlyn. ◆ TRINITY HOUSE NATIONAL LIGHTHOUSE CENTRE - Story of lighthouses. Lighthouse equipment, model ships, buoys, reconstructed lighthouse room. Old Buoy Store, Wharf Road.

ENTERTAINMENT
◆ Cinemas - Causewayhead. Theatres - West Cornwall Arts Centre, Parade Street.
SPORT & LEISURE
◆ Parks & Gardens - Alexandra Grounds, Promenade. Bolitho Gardens, New Road, Newlyn. Morrab Gardens, Morrab Road. Penlee Memorial Park, Morrab Road. St Anthony's Gardens, Battery Road. ◆ Swimming Pools - Jubilee Bathing Pool, Battery Road. ◆ Ten-Pin Bowling - Grand Casino Amusements, Promenade.

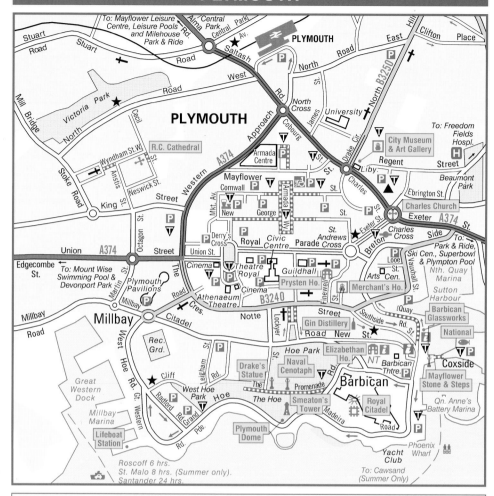

Plymouth is the largest city in the West Country. Associated with sailors such as Hawkins, Raleigh, Frobisher and Sir Francis Drake, the harbour of Plymouth Sound (protected by Rennie's one mile long breakwater of 1812-41), is a safe anchorage leading to the 300 acre Royal Navy Dockyard of Devonport founded in 1691. Pleasure cruises to view the warships depart from the Mayflower Steps and Phoenix Wharf. Much of the city centre (now rebuilt) was destroyed in a bombing raid in 1941, however, the Barbican area, part of the old quarter of Plymouth with narrow streets, survives.

Plymouth Barbican

Drakes Island, Plymouth

PLACES OF INTEREST

Tourist Information Centre (All year) - Island House, The Barbican. Tel: 01752 264849

◆ BARBICAN GLASSWORKS - Glassmaking demonstrations. Visitor centre with information on the maritime & trading history of the Barbican & Sutton Harbour. Old Fishmarket, The Barbican.

◆ CITY MUSEUM & ART GALLERY - Collections of West Country art & porcelain including works by Sir Joshua Reynolds. Natural history. Drake Circus.

◆ CHARLES CHURCH - Bombed building & spire of 17th century church, left as a memorial to Plymouth's war dead. Charles Cross.

◆ DRAKE'S STATUE - Statue of 1884 of Sir Francis Drake overlooking The Hoe, where according to legend he was playing bowls when the Spanish Armada was first sighted in 1588. The Promenade, The Hoe.

◆ ELIZABETHAN HOUSE (NT) - Tudor sea captain's timber framed house. Period furnishings. National Trust Information centre. 32 New Street.

◆ LIFEBOAT STATION - Established in 1803. Arun lifeboat. Millbay Marina, Great Western Road.

◆ MAYFLOWER STONE & STEPS - Memorial stone & steps where the Pilgrim Fathers sailed to America in 1620. The Barbican.

◆ MERCHANT'S HOUSE MUSEUM - 16th century Elizabethan building housing displays on the story of Plymouth including the Eddystone lighthouses, Plymouth's defences & the blitz. Victorian pharmacy. 33 St Andrews Street.

◆ NATIONAL MARINE AQUARIUM - Ocean tank, shark theatre, living coral reef, seawater wave tank & discovery pools. Barbican Approach, Coxside.

◆ NAVAL CENOTAPH - Tall monument commemorating those who died in both world wars. The Promenade, The Hoe.

◆ PLYMOUTH DOME - Life size replica Elizabethan Street. Displays include Plymouth seafarers, blitz devastation & ocean liners. Observation galleries over Plymouth Sound. The Hoe.

◆ PLYMOUTH GIN DISTILLERY - Guided Tours of 200 year old distillery on site of former friary. Audio-visual. Black Friars Distillery, 60 Southside Street.

◆ PLYMOUTH ROMAN CATHOLIC CATHEDRAL - Gothic Revival building of 1858 with 61 m (200 ft) spire. Cecil Street.

◆ PRYSTEN HOUSE - Stone built merchant's town house of 1498. Finewell Street.

◆ ROYAL CITADEL (EH) - Guided tours of England's largest 17th century fortress including Baroque main gate & royal chapel. The Hoe.

◆ SMEATON'S TOWER - Upper part of third Eddystone lighthouse built by John Smeaton in 1759, removed to The Hoe in 1882 when the sea undermined the rock on which it stood. The Hoe.

Smeaton's Tower, The Hoe Plymouth

ENTERTAINMENT

◆ Cinemas - Derry's Cross (two). Plymouth Arts Centre, Looe Street.

◆ Concerts - Plymouth Pavilions, Millbay Road.

◆ Theatres - Athenaeum Theatre, Derry's Cross. Barbican Theatre, Castle St. Theatre Royal, Royal Parade.

SPORT & LEISURE

◆ Ice Rink - Swiss Lake Ice Rink, Plymouth Pavilions, Millbay Road.

◆ Parks & Gardens - Beaumont Park, Tothill Avenue. Central Park, Alma Road. Devonport Park, Exmouth Road, Devonport (W Plymouth Freedom Fields, Lipson Road (E Plymouth). Hoe Park, West Hoe Park & The Hoe. Victoria Park, North Road West.

◆ Ski Slope - Plymouth Ski Centre, Longbridge Road (NE Plymouth).

◆ Sports Centres - Mayflower Leisure Centre, Central Park, Mayflower Drive.

◆ Swimming Pools - Atlantis Pool, Plymouth Pavilions, Millbay Road. Central Park Leisure Pools, Central Park, Mayflower Drive. Mount Wise Swimming Pool, Richmond Walk, Mount Wise (W Plymouth). Plympton Pool, Harewood Park, Plympton (NE of Plymouth). Seaton Pool, Brest Road, Crownhill (N Plymouth).

◆ Ten-Pin Bowling - Plymouth Superbowl, Plymouth Road, Plympton (NE of Plymouth).

St. Ives, formerly one of the most important pilchard fisheries in Cornwall, is now a very popular holiday resort of great charm characterized by the old fishing quarter with its narrow steep cobbled streets, alleys and steps lined with stone cottages. Its setting and clarity of light led to its colonization by artists, notably Ben Nicholson and Barbara Hepworth in 1939. Beyond the harbour, with Smeaton's Pier, is The Island, a headland separating sheltered Porthgwidden Beach from Porthmeor Beach popular for surfing.

PLACES OF INTEREST

Tourist Information Centre (All year) - The Guildhall, Street-an-Pol.
Tel: 01736 796297
◆ BARBARA HEPWORTH MUSEUM & SCULPTURE GARDEN- The artists former workshop displaying over 40 of her sculptures. Trewyn Studios, Barnoon Hill.
◆ LIFEBOAT STATION- Established in 1840. Mersey & Inflatable 'D' lifeboats. West Pier, St. Ives Harbour.

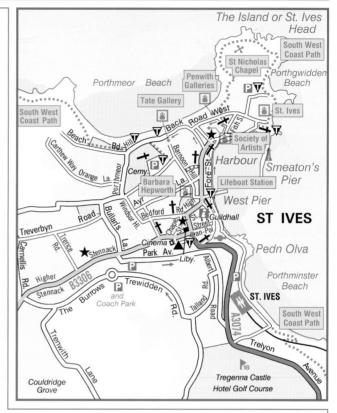

◆ PENWITH GALLERIES- Exhibitions of paintings & sculpture by the Penwith Society of Arts. Back Road West. ◆ ST IVES MUSEUM- Cornish & local history. Displays on fishing, lifeboat, maritime history, railways. Wheal Dream. St. Ives Society of Artists- Paintings & sculptures. Old Mariner's Church, Norway Square. ◆ ST NICHOLAS CHAPEL- Fishermans chapel which exhibited a guiding light prior to the lighthouses on Smeaton's Pier. The Island. ◆ TATE GALLERY ST IVES - Outpost of London's Tate Gallery. Changing displays of 20th century modern art associated with St. Ives & Cornwall. Porthmeor Beach.

ENTERTAINMENT
◆ Cinemas - Royal Square.

SPORT & LEISURE
◆ Parks & Gardens - Trewyn Gardens, Back Street.

St. Ives

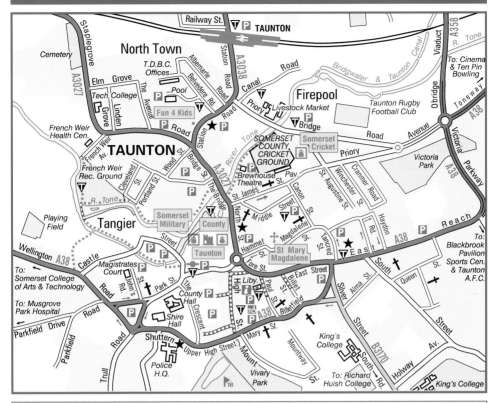

Founded in the 7th century by King Ina to guard the river crossing against the Celts, Taunton, 'the town on the Tone' is the county town of Somerset and home of the county's cricket ground. History has left its mark on the town and the heritage trail highlights many of the towns architectural features using distinctive brass plaques set in the pavement. Buildings of interest include the 14th century Tudor House in Fore Street, the oldest house in Taunton and Gray's Almshouses founded in 1635 by Robert Gray. Taunton developed in the 13th century as an important market and trading town. Today with a population of 60,000, it is still a lively centre with a diverse range of shopping facilities and a livestock market.

PLACES OF INTEREST
Tourist Information Centre (All year) - The Library, Paul Street. Tel: 01823 336344 ◆ FUN 4 KIDS - Action packed all weather attraction for children, includes rope bridges, climbing nets, ball pool & spiral slides. 43 Station Road. ◆ ST MARY MAGDALENE CHURCH - One of the largest & richest perpendicular churches in England. The 49.7m (163ft) tower dating from 1500 was rebuilt in the 19th century & local legend tells of how donkeys were used in the construction to haul the ropes of the pulley system to raise materials to the top. Upon completion of the tower, the donkeys were themselves raised to the top so they could see the view. Magdalene Street. ◆ SOMERSET COUNTY MUSEUM - A wide variety of exhibits are combined to reflect the history of Somerset. The collection includes dolls, toys, silver, pottery, fossils & archaeological items. Taunton Castle, Castle Green. ◆ SOMERSET CRICKET MUSEUM - Housed in a renovated priory barn, this extensive collection of cricket memorabilia reflects the history of the County Club from 1875. Adjacent to the County Cricket Ground. Priory Barn, 7 Priory Avenue. ◆ SOMERSET MILITARY MUSEUM, THE - Exhibition devoted to the history of the Somerset Light Infantry. Somerset County Museum, Taunton Castle, Castle Green. ◆ TAUNTON CASTLE - The remains of the 12th century castle now form part of the County Museum in the town centre. The Great Hall which survives today with some modifications was the scene of Judge Jeffries notorious Bloody Assize held after the collapse of Monmouth's Rebellion in 1685. Castle Green.

ENTERTAINMENT
◆ Cinemas- Heron Gate (E Taunton). Theatres- Brewhouse Theatre & Arts Centre, Coal Orchard.
SPORT & LEISURE
◆ Parks & Gardens - French Weir Park, French Weir Avenue. Goodland Gardens, Castle Street. Victoria Park, Victoria Parkway. Vivary Park, Mount Street.
◆ Sports Centre - Blackbrook Pavilion Sports Centre, Blackbrook Way (SE Taunton).
◆ Swimming Pools - Taunton Pool, Station Road.
◆ Ten Pin Bowling - Hollywood Bowling, Heron Gate (E Taunton).

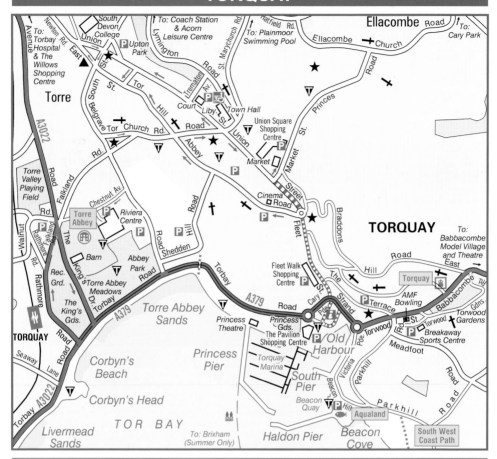

Tor Bay with the three main towns of Torquay, Paignton and Brixham is known as the 'English Riviera' due to the mild climate which supports gardens planted with sub-tropical plants including many palms, similar to those originally imported from New Zealand and the Mediterranean in the early 19th century. The planned streets of the town were first developed by the Cary family of Torre Abbey, the characteristic terraces being built in the first half of the 19th century. The harbour and Torquay Marina provide the focus for the town with the main shopping street of Union Street accessible via Fleet Walk. Torre Abbey Sands, one of over 20 beaches on the Riviera, provides a nearby sandy beach.

PLACES OF INTEREST

Tourist Information Centre (All year)- Vaughan Parade. Tel: 01803 297428

◆ AQUALAND - Largest aquarium in the West. Exotic tropical marine fish & local marine life. Reptiles & birds. Ground floor, multi-storey car park, Beacon Quay, Strand. ◆ TORQUAY MUSEUM - Local history, regimental, archaeology & natural history galleries. Victoriana. Agatha Christie exhibition. 529 Babbacombe Road. ◆ TORRE ABBEY - 18th century house with furnished period rooms, art galleries, chapel, formal gardens on remains of Premonstratensian abbey (founded in 1196) of which the gatehouse, guest hall & tithe (or Spanish) barn survive. The King's Drive.

ENTERTAINMENT

◆ Cinemas - Abbey Road. Theatres - Babbacombe Theatre, Babbacombe Downs, Babbacombe (N of Torquay). Princess Theatre, Torbay Road.

SPORT & LEISURE

◆ Parks & Gardens - Abbey Park (& Torre Abbey Meadows), Torbay Road. Cary Park, Cary Avenue, Babbacombe (N of Torquay). Princess Gardens, Torbay Road. Torwood Gardens, Torwood Gardens Road. Upton Park, Lymington Road. Victoria Park, Sherwell Lane (W Torquay). ◆ Sports Centres - Acorn Leisure Centre, Lichfield Avenue (N Torquay). Breakaway Sports Centre, Torwood Gardens Road. Riviera Centre, Chestnut Avenue. ◆ Swimming Pools - Riviera Centre (as above). Plainmoor Swimming Pool (Swim Torquay), Plainmoor (N of Torquay). ◆ Ten-Pin Bowling - AMF Bowling, Torwood Street.

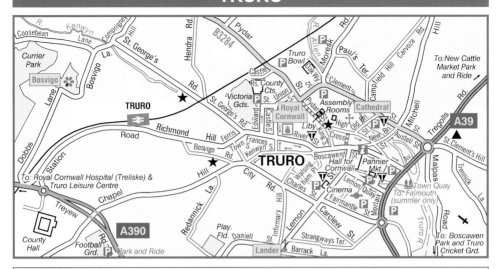

Truro grew up as a tin and copper exporting port on the navigable Truro River, and prospered from becoming a stannary town in the 18th century. Now Cornwall's cathedral city and administrative centre, the city is famous for its Georgian architecture exemplified by Boscawen Street, Strangways Terrace, Walsingham Place and Lemon Street (the finest Georgian Street in Cornwall). Buildings of note are the former Assembly Rooms of 1772 on High Cross and the granite City Hall built in the Italian style. Boat trips to Falmouth operate from Town Quay (or Malpas when the tide is low).

PLACES OF INTEREST
Tourist Information Centre (All year) - Municipal Buildings, City Hall, Boscawen Street. Tel: 01872 274555
◆ BOSVIGO GARDEN - 3 acres of enclosed & walled gardens with herbaceous & rare plants. Bosvigo Lane.
◆ LANDER MONUMENT - Tall granite column with statue of Richard Lander, killed exploring the River Niger
in West Africa. Lemon Street.
◆ ROYAL CORNWALL MUSEUM - Displays include archaeology, local history, mining industry, seafaring, natural history, costumes, fine art. River Street.
◆ TRURO CATHEDRAL - Built between 1880 & 1910 in the Early English style; the first Anglican cathedral to be built in England since the rebuilding of St Paul's and the only cathedral in Cornwall. High Cross.

ENTERTAINMENT
◆ Cinemas - Lemon Street.
◆ Theatres - City Hall, Boscawen Street.

SPORT & LEISURE
◆ Parks & Gardens -
Boscawen Park, Malpas Road (SE of Truro).
Victoria Gardens, Castle Rise.
◆ Sports Centres -
Truro Leisure Centre, College Road (W of Truro).
◆ Swimming Pools -
Truro Leisure Centre (as above).
◆ Ten-Pin Bowling -
Truro Bowl, Oak Way.

Torbay Harbour

BODMIN MOOR

Bodmin Moor, designated an area of outstanding natural beauty, is a remote, bleak heather covered upland granite moorland bisected by the main A30 road and still grazed by moorland ponies. Similar, but smaller and lower than Dartmoor, it was densely populated in the bronze age and has many archaeological remains. The best known are the three stone circles of The Hurlers, Rillaton Barrow and the hill fort of Stowe's Pound all near Minions, and the Stripple Stones Henge and Trippet Stone Circle on Hawkstor Downs near Blisland.

Natural features include Brown Willy, at 420 m (1,377 ft), the highest point on both Bodmin Moor and in Cornwall, and the rockier Roughtor, the second highest point, readily accesible from Camelford with over seventy hut circles on its north west slope. The Cheesewring, at Stowe's Hill near Minions, is a popular wind eroded granite formation of circular stones balanced on top of each other whilst the natural lake of Dozmary Pool, in the centre of the moor south of Bolventor, is according to legend where Sir Bedivere threw King Arthur's Sword Excalibur. Also at Bolventor is Jamaica Inn featured in the novel of the same name by Daphne du Maurier with Smugglers tableaux, memorial room, and Potter's Museum of Curiosity displaying over 10,000 stuffed animals.

Ruins of tin and copper mines can be seen to the south east of the moor at Minions and include the ruined engine houses of the Phoenix United and South Phoenix Mines. The Minions Heritage Centre is in Houseman's Engine House. Other attractions include Golitha Falls, managed by English Nature at the southern edge of the moor near Redgate and Wesley Cottage at Trewint, near Altarnun, where John Wesley, the founder of Methodism, stayed. There are reservoirs at Colliford Lake and Siblyback Lake Water Park.

Bodmin Moor

DARTMOOR

Dartmoor, one of the last great wildernesses of southern England, is a 365 square mile bleak granite upland with an average elevation of 366 m (1200 ft), designated a National Park in 1951. It is characterized by its coarse granite outcrops, or tors, and by large areas of isolated blanket peat bog covered with purple gorse and heather which provide rough grazing for the semi-wild Dartmoor ponies. The rapidly changing weather conditions, frequently with low cloud, heavy rain and fog, provided the setting for Conan Doyle's novel 'The Hound of the Baskervilles'. The heart of the moorland is crossed by only two significant roads meeting at Two Bridges, near Princetown with its infamous prison of 1806 the only town of any size. Remains of mining can be found at the Vitifer Tin Mine and the Wheal Betsy Pumping Engine House at Mary Tavy. Granite quarrying developed in the 19th century, the largest quarries were at Haytor and Foggintor (where stone for Nelson's Column in London was quarried).

The moor was extensively farmed in the bronze age when the climate was milder, and is covered in prehistoric remains such as the Merrivale Prehistoric Settlement, Grimspound near Postbridge and the remote Stall Moor and Butterdon stone rows. The moor has many medieval stone clapper bridges examples being at Postbridge, Bellever and Dartmeet.

The Ministry of Defence training area in the north part of the moor (with live firing- observe warning signs), has the two highest points of High Willhays (621 m, 2038 ft) and Yes Tor (619 m, 2030 ft). Other tors to the west of the moor are Great Staple Tor, Great Mis Tor and Vixen Tor, with a sphynx like profile, the tallest rock pile on Dartmoor at 27 m (90 ft) from base to top, near Merrivale. Hound Tor, with its deserted medieval village, the popular Haytor Rocks, with its granite tramway and Blackingstone Rock, 24 m (80 ft) above ground level with Victorian iron steps, are in the east.

There are many beauty spots in the river valleys around the edge of the moor. In the east is Fingle Bridge (near the famous Castle Drogo), Lustleigh Cleave, Becky Falls and Canonteign Falls near Hennock comprising Lady Exmouth Falls, at 67 m (220 ft) England's highest waterfall. In the west is Lydford Gorge and the more open Tavy Cleave. To the south is the Dewerstone Rock; the 50 m (165 ft) high crags form the finest rock climbing face in inland Devon. The granite 'chimney' Bowerman's Nose is near Manaton and the intriguing Ten Commandments Stone is at Buckland in the Moor.

EXMOOR (see also Lynton and Lynmouth description)

Exmoor is mainly defined by the 267 square miles of the Exmoor National Park created in 1954. Comprising a plateau of sedimentary rocks and slate regularly reaching 400 m (1312 ft), it does not have the rugged granite tors of Bodmin Moor and Dartmoor, but is more remote and less crowded. The western edge rises sharply whilst the Brendon Hills to the east have the gentlest contours. The 30 square mile Exmoor Forest at Simonsbath (never in fact forested), were once a royal deer park. The area typifies the bleak upland moorland with coarse grass, bracken, heather and gorse especially seen at The Chains, a waterlogged wilderness forming the head waters of the Exe, Barle and West Lyn rivers.

Deep thickly wooded valleys make up the lower sections of the moor, many of which are accessible only by walking. Heddon's Cleave (200 m, 656 ft deep), is reached by footpath from Hunter's Inn, Badgworthy Water from Malmsmead, and Horner Wood (at 900 acre, one of the largest ancient oak woodlands in the country), by trails through the valley of Horner Water. Accessible by car is the National Trust owned Watersmeet, a popular beauty spot at the junction of the steep wooded valleys of the East Lyn River and Hoaroak Water east of Lynmouth.

There is spectacular scenery on the coast with a series of headlands interrupted only by the Vale of Porlock. Notable are the cliffs at Countisbury, at around 137 m (450 ft) the highest in Devon, and the striking Little Hangman near Combe Martin.

Exmoor is well known for large numbers of red deer and the native Exmoor ponies. Oare Church and Robber's Bridge are famous for their associations with R.D. Blackmore's novel 'Lorna Doone'. Doone Valley (actually Hoccombe Combe) is reached either by a 2 mile walk from Malmsmead along the valley of Badgworthy Water (which runs along the Devon Somerset border), or across Brendon Common.

Tarr Steps over the River Barle (at 55 m or 180 ft long with 17 spans), is the finest example of a clapper bridge in the country (best approached from the B3223 at Winsford Hill), Landacre Bridge is a preserved medieval bridge in a moorland setting near Withypool Common, whilst the scenic Bury Packhorse Bridge is near Dulverton. Exmoor's tallest standing stone, the 3 m (9 ft) high Longstone, and Chapman Barrows bronze age burial mounds, are near Challacombe. Dunkery Beacon at 519 m (1704 ft) is the highest point on Exmoor and in Somerset, whilst Western Common, near Kinsford Gate, at 493 m (1617 ft) is the highest point on Exmoor within Devon. From here, a desolate road follows the ridge along the Somerset border south east for 9 miles to West Anstey Common where the 13 ton Hancock Memorial Stone was erected in 1935 in memory of a local hunter. Other notable places are Culbone Church, near Porlock with its scenic toll roads, thought to be the smallest complete parish church in England and the town of Dunster, famous for its castle and gardens and early 17th century octagonal Yarn Market.

Portchapel Beach, Cornwall

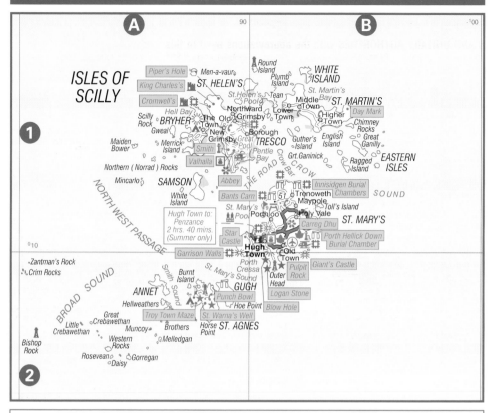

Tourist Information Centre (All year) - The Old Wesleyan Chapel, Garrison Lane, Hugh Town, St Mary's. Tel: 01720 422536

The Isles of Scilly, an archipelago of about 150 granite islands, islets and rocks, 28 miles south west of Land's End, are according to legend, the only visible relic of Lyonesse, the land of Arthurian legend. The islands have many bronze age cairns and iron age remains. With a very mild climate, the chief industry outside tourism is floriculture, with spring flowers grown in tiny sheltered fields being exported as early as November. The five largest islands are populated- St Mary's, Tresco, Bryher, St Martin's and St Agnes. Seals and seabirds abound on the many uninhabited islands and the autumn migration of both sea and land birds is renowned. Hugh Town, St Mary's where launches leave to all the off islands, is reached by ferry and helicopter from Penzance and plane from Land's End Aerodrome (St Just).

St Mary's is the largest island with most of the population centred on the capital Hugh Town, situated on the isthmus to The Garrison peninsula fortified by a 1.5 mile long granite wall and Star Castle (now a hotel). The Isles of Scilly Museum is in Church Street. To the north of the island are the bronze age Bant's Carn Burial Chamber and Halangy Down Ancient Village. On the south coast Old Town Bay churchyard has the graves of 120 people lost in the wreck of the German trans-atlantic liner 'Schiller' in 1875 and Porth Hellick has a monument to Rear-Admiral Sir Cloudesley Shovell lost with the Association and three other ships in 1707 on the Western Rocks. Peninnis Head has the overhanging Pulpit Rock, Logan Stone weighing over 300 tons, and many naturally eroded granite shapes. Telegraph Hill is the highest point on St Mary's and Scilly at 51 m (167 ft).

Tresco is famous for its Tresco Abbey sub-tropical Gardens, on the site of a 12th century benedictine priory (of which an archway survives), and the Valhalla Collection of 19th century ships figureheads from vessels lost around the islands. The contrasting rugged north end of the island beyond New Grimsby has King Charles's Castle, the 17th century Cromwell's Castle, the Old Blockhouse harbour gun tower at Old Grimsby and Piper's Hole, a natural cave with pool.

Bryher is noted for the rocky coast at Shipman Head and Hell Bay on the wild northern part of the island.

St Martin's is known for its fine beaches on the south side. A large pepper pot navigation mark- the Day Mark of 1685, is on Chapel Down on the east tip. St Agnes has the Troy Town Maze on the Downs, set in pebbles by an 18th century keeper of St Agnes Lighthouse (built 1680 and disused in 1911), the second oldest surviving purpose built lighthouse in the country. Also of note is the the Punch Bowl, a curiously perched boulder on Wingletang Down. 4 miles south west, past the bird sanctuary on Annet, is Bishop Rock Lighthouse (built in 1858 and rebuilt in 1887) one of Britain's tallest lighthouses guarding the treacherous waters around the Western Rocks.

INDEX TO CITIES, TOWNS, VILLAGES, HAMLETS & LOCATIONS.

1) A strict alphabetical order is used e.g. Ash Thomas follows Ashrelghney but precedes Ashton.

2) The map reference given refers to the actual map square in which the town spot or built-up area is located and not to the place name.

3) Where two or more places of the same name occur in the same County or Unitary Authority, the nearest large town is also given; e.g. Aish. *Devn* —1A **16** (nr. South Brent) indicates that Aish is located in square 1A on page **16** and is situated near South Brent in the County of Devon.

COUNTIES AND UNITARY AUTHORITIES with the abbreviations used in this index.

Cornwall : *Corn*
Devon : *Devn*
Dorset : *Dors*
Isles of Scilly : *IOS*
North Somerset : *N Som*
Plymouth : *Plym*
Somerset : *Som*

INDEX

Abbey. *Devn* —2B **30**
Abbey Gate. *Devn* —1C **25**
Abbots Bickington. *Devn* —2B **26**
Abbotsham. *Devn* —1C **27**
Abbotskerswell. *Devn* —1C **17**
Abbotsleigh. *Devn* —3C **17**
Addington. *Corn* —1A **14**
Adsborough. *Som* —1C **31**
Adscombe. *Som* —3B **36**
Afton. *Devn* —1C **17**
Aish. *Devn* —1A **16** (nr. South Brent)
Aish. *Devn* —2C **17** (nr. Stoke Gabriel)
Aisholt. *Som* —3B **36**
Albaston. *Corn* —3C **21**
Alcombe. *Som* —2D **35**
Aley. *Som* —3B **36**
Alfardisworthy. *Devn* —2A **26**
Alfington. *Devn* —1B **24**
Allaleigh. *Devn* —2C **17**
Aller. *Devn* —1B **28**
Aller. *Som* —1D **31**
Allercombe. *Devn* —1A **24**
Allerford. *Som* —2D **35** (nr. Minehead)
Allerford. *Som* —1B **30** (nr. Taunton)
Allet. *Corn* —3D **11**
Allowenshay. *Som* —2D **31**
Alminstone Cross. *Devn* —1B **26**
Alphington. *Devn* —2D **23**
Alstone. *Som* —2D **37**
Alston Sutton. *Som* —1D **37**
Alswear. *Devn* —1B **28**
Altarnun. *Corn* —2A **20**
Alverdiscott. *Devn* —1D **27**
Alwington. *Devn* —1C **27**
Andersea. *Som* —3D **37**
Andersfield. *Som* —3C **37**
Angarrack. *Corn* —2C **7**
Angarrick. *Corn* —1B **8**
Antony. *Corn* —2B **14**
Antron. *Corn* —3D **7**
Anvil Corner. *Devn* —3B **26**
Appledore. *Devn* —3C **33** (nr. Bideford)
Appledore. *Devn* —2A **30** (nr. Tiverton)
Appley. *Som* —1A **30**
Arlington. *Devn* —2A **34**
Arlington Beccott. *Devn* —2A **34**
Ascott. *Devn* —3A **34**
Ashbrittle. *Som* —1A **30**
Ashburton. *Devn* —1B **16**
Ashbury. *Devn* —1D **21**
Ashcombe. *Devn* —3D **23**
Ashcott. *Som* —3D **37**
Ashculme. *Devn* —2B **30**
Ashford. *Devn* —3A **16** (nr. Aveton Gifford)
Ashford. *Devn* —3D **33** (nr. Barnstaple)
Ashill. *Devn* —2A **30**
Ashill. *Som* —2D **31**
Ashley. *Devn* —2D **29**
Ashmansworthy. *Devn* —2B **26**
Ashmill. *Devn* —1B **20** (nr. Ashwater)
Ash Mill. *Devn* —1B **28** (nr. Bishop's Nympton)
Ash Moor. *Devn* —2B **28**
Ashprington. *Devn* —2C **17**
Ash Priors. *Som* —1B **30**
Ashrelghney. *Devn* —2A **28**
Ash Thomas. *Devn* —2A **30**
Ashton. *Corn* —3D **7** (nr. Breage)
Ashton. *Corn* —1B **14** (nr. Callington)
Ashwater. *Devn* —1B **20**
Athelney. *Som* —1D **31**
Atherington. *Devn* —1D **27**
Aunk. *Devn* —3A **30**
Avercombe. *Devn* —1B **28**
Aveton Gifford. *Devn* —3A **16**
Avonwick. *Devn* —2B **16**
Awliscombe. *Devn* —3B **30**
Axbridge. *Som* —1D **37**
Axminster. *Devn* —1D **25**
Axmouth. *Devn* —1C **25**
Axtown. *Devn* —1D **15**
Aylesbeare. *Devn* —1A **24**
Aylescott. *Devn* —2A **28**
Ayshford. *Devn* —2A **30**

Babbacombe. *Devn* —1D **17**
Badgall. *Corn* —2A **20**
Badgworth. *Som* —1D **37**
Badharlick. *Corn* —2A **20**
Bampton. *Devn* —1D **29**
Bankland. *Som* —1D **31**
Banwell. *N Som* —1D **37**
Barbrook. *Devn* —2B **34**
Bareppa. *Corn* —2B **8**
Barkia Shop. *Corn* —2D **11**
Barrington. *Som* —2D **31**
Barripper. *Corn* —2D **7**
Barton. *N Som* —1D **37**
Barton Town. *Devn* —2A **34**
Barwick. *Devn* —3D **27**
Bason Bridge. *Som* —2D **37**
Bathealton. *Som* —1A **30**
Bathpool. *Corn* —3A **20**
Bathpool. *Som* —1C **31**
Battisborough Cross. *Devn* —3D **15**
Battleborough. *Som* —1D **37**
Battledown Cross. *Devn* —3C **27**
Battleton. *Som* —1D **29**
Bawdrip. *Som* —3D **37**
Beacon. *Devn* —3B **30**
Beaford. *Devn* —2D **27**
Bealbury. *Corn* —1B **14**
Bealsmill. *Corn* —3B **20**
Beardon. *Devn* —2D **21**
Beaston. *Devn* —1B **16**
Beaworthy. *Devn* —1C **21**
Beeny. *Corn* —1D **19**
Beer. *Devn* —2C **25**
Beer. *Som* —3D **37**
Beer Crocombe. *Som* —1D **31**
Beesands. *Devn* —3C **17**
Beeson. *Devn* —3C **17**
Beethham. *Som* —2C **31**
Beggearn Huish. *Som* —3A **36**
Bellever. *Devn* —3A **22**
Belowda. *Corn* —1B **12**
Belstone. *Devn* —1A **22**
Belstone Corner. *Devn* —1A **22**
Bennacott. *Corn* —1A **20**
Bennah. *Devn* —2C **23**
Benny Mill. *Corn* —2A **12**
Bere Alston. *Devn* —1C **15**
Bere Ferrers. *Devn* —1C **15**
Berepper. *Corn* —3D **7**
Berriowbridge. *Corn* —3A **20**
Berrow. *Som* —1C **37**
Berry Cross. *Devn* —2C **27**
Berrydown. *Devn* —2A **22**
Berry Down Cross. *Devn* —2D **33**
Berrynarbor. *Devn* —2D **33**
Berry Pomeroy. *Devn* —1C **17**
Bethel. *Corn* —2C **13**
Bettiscombe. *Dors* —3D **31**
Bickenhall. *Som* —2C **31**
Bickington. *Devn* —3D **33** (nr. Barnstaple)
Bickington. *Devn* —3B **22** (nr. Newton Abbot)
Bickleigh. *Devn* —1D **15** (nr. Plymouth)
Bickleigh. *Devn* —3D **29** (nr. Tiverton)
Bickleton. *Devn* —3D **33**
Bicknoller. *Som* —3B **36**
Biddisham. *Som* —1D **37**
Bideford. *Devn* —1C **27**
Bidlake. *Devn* —2C **21**
Bigbury. *Devn* —3A **16**
Bigbury-on-Sea. *Devn* —3A **16**
Bilbrook. *Som* —2A **36**
Billacombe. *Plym* —2D **15**
Billacott. *Corn* —1A **20**
Birchwood. *Som* —2C **31**
Birdsmoorgate. *Dors* —3D **31**
Birthem Bottom. *Devn* —2A **30**
Biscovey. *Corn* —2C **13**
Bish Mill. *Devn* —1B **28**
Bishop's Hull. *Som* —1C **31**
Bishops Lydeard. *Som* —1B **30**
Bishop's Nympton. *Devn* —1B **28**
Bishop's Tawton. *Devn* —3D **33**
Bishopsteignton. *Devn* —3D **23**
Bishopswood. *Som* —2C **31**
Bissoe. *Corn* —3D **11**
Bittadon *Devn* —2D **33**
Bittaford. *Devn* —2A **16**
Blackawton. *Devn* —2C **17**
Blackborough. *Devn* —3A **30**
Black Cross. *Corn* —1B **12**
Black Dog. *Devn* —3C **29**
Blackdown. *Dors* —3D **31**
Blackford. *Som* —2D **37**
Blackmoor Gate. *Devn* —2A **34**
Blackney. *Dors* —1D **25**
Blackpool. *Devn* —3C **17**
Black Torrington. *Devn* —3C **27**
Blackwater. *Corn* —3D **11**
Blackwater. *Som* —2C **31**
Blackwell. *Som* —1A **30**
Blagden Hill. *Som* —2C **31**
Blagdon. *Devn* —1C **17**
Bleadon. *N Som* —1D **37**
Blisland. *Corn* —3D **19**
Blowinghouse. *Corn* —2D **11**
Blue Anchor. *Corn* —2B **12**
Blunts. *Corn* —1B **14**
Boasley Cross. *Devn* —1C **21**
Bocaddon. *Corn* —2D **13**
Boconnoc. *Corn* —1D **13**
Bodieve. *Corn* —3B **18**
Bodilly. *Corn* —2D **7**
Bodiniel. *Corn* —1C **13**
Bodinnick. *Corn* —2D **13**
Bodmin. *Corn* —1C **13**
Bodwen. *Corn* —1C **13**
Bofamel. *Corn* —1D **13**
Bogtown. *Devn* —1C **21**
Bohetherick. *Corn* —1C **15**
Bohortha. *Corn* —1C **9**
Bojewyan. *Corn* —2A **6**
Bokiddick. *Corn* —1C **13**
Bolenowe. *Corn* —2D **7**
Bolham. *Devn* —2D **29**
Bolham Water. *Devn* —2B **30**
Bollingey. *Corn* —2D **11**
Bolventor. *Corn* —3D **19**
Bondleigh. *Devn* —3A **28**
Bonehill. *Devn* —3B **22**
Boode. *Devn* —3D **33**
Boreston. *Devn* —2B **16**
Borough. *Devn* —3A **26**
Borough. *IOS* —1A **66**
Borough Cross. *Devn* —2C **33**
Bosavern. *Corn* —2A **6**
Boscarne. *Corn* —1C **13**
Boscastle. *Corn* —1C **19**
Boscoppa. *Corn* —2C **13**
Boskenna. *Corn* —3B **6**
Bosoughan. *Corn* —1A **12**
Bossiney. *Corn* —2C **19**
Bossington. *Som* —2C **35**
Boswarthen. *Corn* —2B **6**
Boswinger. *Corn* —3B **12**
Botallack. *Corn* —2A **6**
Botternell. *Corn* —3A **20**
Bottoms. *Corn* —3A **6**
Botusfleming. *Corn* —1C **15**
Bovey Tracey. *Devn* —3C **23**
Bow. *Devn* —3B **28**
Bowd. *Devn* —1B **24**
Bowden. *Devn* —3C **17**
Bowithick. *Corn* —2D **19**
Bowling Green. *Corn* —3B **20**
Box's Shop. *Corn* —3A **26**
Boyton. *Corn* —1B **20**
Braddock. *Corn* —1D **13**
Bradfield. *Devn* —3A **30**
Bradford. *Corn* —3D **19**
Bradford. *Devn* —3C **27**
Bradford Barton. *Devn* —2C **29**
Bradford-on-Tone. *Som* —1B **30**
Bradiford. *Devn* —3D **33**
Bradley Green. *Som* —3C **37**
Bradney. *Som* —3D **37**
Bradninch. *Devn* —3D **29**
Bradstone. *Devn* —2B **20**
Bradworthy. *Devn* —2B **26**
Brampford Speke. *Devn* —1D **23**
Brandls Corner. *Devn* —3C **27**
Brandninch. *Devn* —3A **34**
Branscombe. *Devn* —2B **24**
Bratton Clovelly. *Devn* —1C **21**
Bratton Fleming. *Devn* —3A **34**
Braunton. *Devn* —3C **33**
Brayford. *Devn* —3A **34**
Brayfordhill. *Devn* —3A **34**
Bray Shop. *Corn* —3B **20**
Brazacott. *Corn* —1A **20**
Breage. *Corn* —3D **7**
Brean. *Som* —1C **37**
Brendon. *Devn* —2B **26** (nr. Bradworthy)
Brendon. *Devn* —2B **34** (nr. Lynton)
Brent Knoll. *Som* —1D **37**
Brenton. *Devn* —2D **23**
Bridestowe. *Devn* —2D **21**
Bridford. *Devn* —2C **23**
Bridfordmills. *Devn* —2C **23**
Bridge. *Corn* —1D **7**
Bridge Ball. *Devn* —2B **34**
Bridge End. *Devn* —3A **16**
Bridgend. *Devn* —3D **15**
Bridge Reeve. *Devn* —2A **28**
Bridgerule. *Devn* —3A **26**
Bridges. *Corn* —2C **13**
Bridgetown. *Corn* —2B **20**
Bridgtetown. *Som* —3D **35**
Bridgwater. *Som* —3C **37**
Brightley. *Devn* —1D **21**
Brighton. *Corn* —2B **12**
Brightor. *Corn* —1B **14**
Brill. *Corn* —2B **8**
Brimley. *Devn* —3B **22**
Brinscombe. *Som* —1D **37**
Brinsea. *N Som* —1D **37**
Brixham. *Devn* —2D **17**
Brixton. *Devn* —2D **15**
Broadclyst. *Devn* —1D **23**
Broadhembury. *Devn* —3B **30**
Broadhempston. *Devn* —1C **17**
Broad Lane. *Corn* —1D **7**
Broadleigh. *Som* —2A **30**
Broad Oak. *Devn* —1A **24**
Broadoak. *Dors* —1D **25**
Broadshard. *Som* —2D **31**
Broadway. *Som* —2D **31**
Broadwindsor. *Dors* —3D **31**
Broadwoodkelly. *Devn* —3A **28**
Broadwoodwidger. *Devn* —2C **21**
Brocton. *Corn* —1C **13**
Brompton Ralph. *Som* —3A **36**
Brompton Regis. *Som* —3D **35**
Brook. *Devn* —3C **21**
Broomfield. *Som* —3C **37**
Brownston. *Devn* —2A **16**
Brownstone. *Devn* —3B **28**
Brushford. *Devn* —3A **28**
Brushford. *Som* —1D **29**
Brynsworthy. *Devn* —3D **33**
Buckerell. *Devn* —3B **30**
Buckfast. *Devn* —1B **16**
Buckfastleigh. *Devn* —1B **16**
Buckland. *Devn* —3A **16**
Buckland Brewer. *Devn* —1C **27**
Buckland Filleigh. *Devn* —3C **27**
Buckland in the Moor. *Devn* —3B **22**
Buckland Monachorum. *Devn* —1C **15**
Buckland St Mary. *Som* —2C **31**
Buckland-Tout-Saints. *Devn* —3B **16**
Buckleigh. *Devn* —1C **27**
Buck's Cross. *Devn* —1B **26**
Buckshead. *Corn* —3A **12**
Buck's Mills. *Devn* —1B **26**
Bude. *Corn* —3A **26**
Budge's Shop. *Corn* —2B **14**
Budgett's Cross. *Som* —2B **30**
Budlake. *Devn* —3D **29**
Budleigh Salterton. *Devn* —2A **24**
Budock Water. *Corn* —1B **8**
Bugle. *Corn* —2C **13**
Bulkworthy. *Devn* —2B **26**
Bulstone. *Devn* —2B **24**
Bulverton. *Devn* —2B **24**
Bunneford Cross. *Devn* —3D **29**
Burlawn. *Corn* —3B **18**
Burlescombe. *Devn* —2A **30**
Burlestone. *Devn* —3C **17**
Burnham-on-Sea. *Som* —2D **37**
Burras. *Corn* —2D **7**
Burraton. *Corn* —2C **15**
Burridge. *Devn* —3D **31**
Burrington. *Devn* —2A **28**
Burrow. *Devn* —2A **24**
Burrow. *Som* —2D **35**
Burrowbridge. *Som* —3D **37**
Burstock. *Dors* —3D **31**
Burston. *Devn* —3B **28**
Burtle. *Som* —2D **37**
Burton. *Som* —2B **36**
Burwood. *Devn* —2D **27**
Bury. *Som* —1D **29**
Buscaverran. *Corn* —2D **7**
Bush. *Corn* —3A **26**
Bussex. *Som* —3D **37**
Butterleigh. *Devn* —3D **29**
Bystock. *Devn* —2A **24**

Cabbacott. *Devn* —1C **27**
Cadbury. *Devn* —3D **29**
Cadeleigh. *Devn* —3D **29**
Cadgwith. *Corn* —3B **8**
Calenick. *Corn* —3A **12**
Callestick. *Corn* —2D **11**
Callington. *Corn* —1B **14**
Calstock. *Corn* —1C **15**
Calverleigh. *Devn* —2D **29**
Camborne. *Corn* —1D **7**
Cambrose. *Corn* —1D **7**
Camelford. *Corn* —2D **19**
Camp. *Devn* —1D **21**
Cannington. *Som* —3C **37**
Canonstown. *Corn* —2C **7**

Visitors' Devon & Cornwall Atlas 67

Kestle Mill—Nine Oaks

Kestle Mill. *Corn* —2A **12**
Kewstoke. *N Som* —1D **37**
Kilkhampton. *Corn* —2A **26**
Killington. *Devn* —2A **34**
Kilmington. *Devn* —1C **25**
Kilton. *Som* —2B **36**
Kilve. *Som* —2B **36**
Kingford. *Devn* —2A **28**
Kingsand. *Corn* —2C **15**
Kingsbridge. *Devn* —3B **16**
Kingsbridge. *Som* —3D **35**
Kingsbury Episcopi. *Som* —1D **31**
Kingscott. *Devn* —2D **27**
Kingsdon. *Devn* —1C **25**
Kingskerswell. *Devn* —1C **17**
Kingsteignton. *Devn* —3C **23**
Kingston. *Devn* —2A **24**
(nr. Colaton Raleigh)
Kingston. *Devn* —2D **17**
(nr. Kingswear)
Kingston. *Devn* —3A **16**
(nr. Ringmore)
Kingstone. *Som* —2D **31**
Kingston St Mary. *Som* —1C **31**
Kingswear. *Devn* —2C **17**
Kingswood. *Som* —3B **36**
Kittisford. *Som* —1A **30**
Kittisford Barton. *Som* —1A **30**
Knapp. *Som* —1D **31**
Knightacott. *Devn* —3A **34**
Knightcott. *N Som* —1D **37**
Knighton. *Devn* —3D **15**
Knighton. *Som* —2B **36**
Knowle. *Devn* —1B **16**
(nr. Ashburton)
Knowle. *Devn* —3C **33**
(nr. Braunton)
Knowle. *Devn* —3A **30**
(nr. Collompton)
Knowle. *Devn* —3B **28**
(nr. Copplestone)
Knowle. *Devn* —2A **24**
(nr. Exmouth)
Knowle Cross. *Devn* —1A **24**
Knowle St Giles. *Som* —2D **31**
Knowstone. *Devn* —1C **29**
Kuggar. *Corn* —3B **8**

Ladock. *Corn* —2A **12**
Ladycross. *Corn* —2B **20**
Lake. *Devn* —3D **33**
(nr. Barnstaple)
Lake. *Devn* —3C **27**
(nr. Chilla)
Lamellion. *Corn* —1A **14**
Lamerton. *Devn* —3C **21**
Lamorick. *Corn* —1C **13**
Lamorna. *Corn* —3B **6**
Lamorran. *Corn* —3A **12**
Lampen. *Corn* —1D **13**
Lana. *Devn* —1B **20**
(nr. Nethercott)
Lana. *Devn* —3B **26**
(nr. Pancrasweek)
Lanarth. *Corn* —2B **8**
Landcross. *Devn* —1C **27**
Landkey. *Devn* —3D **33**
Landkey Newland. *Devn* —3D **33**
Landrake. *Corn* —1B **14**
Landscove. *Devn* —1B **16**
Landulph. *Corn* —1C **15**
Lane. *Corn* —1A **12**
Laneast. *Corn* —2A **20**
Langaford. *Devn* —1C **21**
Langarth. *Corn* —3D **11**
Langdon. *Corn* —1A **20**
Langdon Cross. *Corn* —2B **20**
Langford. *Devn* —1D **23**
(nr. Exeter)
Langford. *Devn* —3A **30**
(nr. Plymtree)
Langford Barton. *Corn* —3A **26**
Langford Barton. *Devn* —2A **16**
Langley. *Som* —1A **30**
Langley Marsh. *Som* —1A **30**
Langore. *Corn* —2A **20**
Langport. *Som* —1D **31**
Langridgeford. *Devn* —1D **27**
Langtree. *Devn* —2C **27**
Lanivet. *Corn* —1C **13**
Lanjeth. *Corn* —2B **12**
Lank. *Corn* —3C **19**
Lanlivery. *Corn* —2C **13**
Lanner. *Corn* —1B **8**
Lanreath. *Corn* —2D **13**
Lansallos. *Corn* —2D **13**
Lanteglos Highway. *Corn* —2D **13**
Lapford. *Devn* —3B **28**
Larkbeare. *Devn* —1A **24**
Larrick. *Corn* —3B **20**
Latchley. *Corn* —3C **21**
Laughton Budville. *Som* —1B **30**
Launcells Cross. *Corn* —3A **26**
Launceston. *Corn* —2B **20**
Lawhitton. *Corn* —2B **20**
Laymore. *Dors* —3D **31**
Ledstone. *Devn* —3B **16**
Lee. *Devn* —2C **33**
(nr. Ilfracombe)
Lee. *Devn* —1C **29**
(nr. Molland)
Leedstown. *Corn* —2D **7**
Leeford. *Devn* —2B **34**
Lee Mill. *Devn* —2D **15**
Lee Moor. *Devn* —1D **15**
Leigham. *Plym* —2D **15**
Leighland Chapel. *Som* —3A **36**
Lelant. *Corn* —2C **7**
Lelant Downs. *Corn* —2C **7**
Lerryn. *Corn* —2D **13**
Lesnewth. *Corn* —1D **19**
Lettaford. *Devn* —2B **22**
Leusdon. *Devn* —3B **22**
Levalsa Meor. *Corn* —3C **13**
Lewannick. *Corn* —2A **20**
Lewdon. *Devn* —2C **21**
Leworthy. *Devn* —3A **34**
(nr. Bratton Fleming)
Leworthy. *Devn* —3B **26**
(nr. Holsworthy)
Lewthorn Cross. *Devn* —3B **22**
Lewtrenchard. *Devn* —2C **21**
Ley. *Corn* —1D **13**
Lezant. *Corn* —3B **20**
Lezerea. *Corn* —2D **7**
Lidwell. *Corn* —3B **20**
Lifton. *Devn* —2B **20**
Liftondown. *Devn* —2B **20**
Lilstock. *Som* —2B **36**
Linkinhorne. *Corn* —3B **20**
Liscombe. *Som* —3C **35**
Liskeard. *Corn* —1A **14**
Little Comfort. *Corn* —2B **20**
Little Croft West. *Corn* —3D **11**
Littleham. *Devn* —2A **24**
(nr. Exmouth)
Littleham. *Devn* —1C **27**
(nr. Saltrens)
Littlehampton. *Devn* —1C **17**
Little Petherick. *Corn* —3B **18**
Little Potheridge. *Devn* —2D **27**
Little Silver. *Devn* —3D **29**
Little Torrington. *Devn* —2C **27**
Littlewindsor. *Dors* —3D **31**
Liverton. *Devn* —3C **23**
Livingshayes. *Devn* —3D **29**
Lizard. *Corn* —3B **8**
Llsington. *Devn* —3B **22**
Lobb. *Devn* —3C **33**
Lobhillcross. *Devn* —2C **21**
Lockengate. *Corn* —1C **13**
Locking. *N Som* —1D **37**
Loddiswell. *Devn* —3B **16**
London Apprentice. *Corn* —2C **13**
Longbridge. *Plym* —2D **15**
Longcombe. *Devn* —2C **17**
Longdown. *Devn* —1C **23**
Longdowns. *Corn* —1B **8**
Longrock. *Corn* —2C **7**
Longstone. *Corn* —3C **19**
Looe. *Corn* —2A **14**
Lopen. *Som* —2D **31**
Lostwithiel. *Corn* —2D **13**
Lower Amble. *Corn* —3B **18**
Lower Ashton. *Devn* —2C **23**
Lower Boscaswell. *Corn* —2A **6**
Lower Cheriton. *Devn* —3B **30**
Lower Dean. *Devn* —1B **16**
Lower Eype. *Dors* —1D **25**
Lower Gabwell. *Devn* —1D **17**
Lower Godsworthy. *Devn* —3D **21**
Lower Lanherne. *Corn* —1A **12**
Lower Lovacott. *Devn* —1D **27**
Lower Loxhore. *Devn* —3A **34**
Lower Roadwater. *Som* —3A **36**
Lower Slade. *Devn* —2D **33**
Lower Tale. *Devn* —3A **30**
Lowertown. *Corn* —3D **7**
Lower Town. *Devn* —3B **22**
(nr. Ashburton)
Lowertown. *Devn* —2C **21**
(nr. Stowford)
Lower Town. *IOS* —1B **66**
Lower Twitchen. *Devn* —2B **26**
Lower Vexford. *Som* —3B **36**
Lower Weare. *Som* —1D **37**
Low Ham. *Som* —1D **31**
Lowton. *Devn* —3A **28**
Lowton. *Som* —2B **30**
Loxbeare *Devn* —2D **29**
Loxhore. *Devn* —3A **34**
Loxton. *N Som* —1D **37**
Luccombe. *Som* —2D **35**
Luckett. *Corn* —3B **20**
Luckwell Bridge. *Som* —3D **35**
Ludgvan. *Corn* —2C **7**
Luffincott. *Devn* —1B **20**
Luppitt. *Devn* —3B **30**
Lupridge. *Devn* —2B **16**
Luscombe. *Devn* —2B **16**
Luson. *Devn* —2A **16**
Lustleigh. *Devn* —2B **22**
Luton. *Devn* —3D **23**
(nr. Ideford)
Luton. *Devn* —3A **30**
(nr. Payhembury)
Lutsford. *Devn* —2A **26**
Lutton. *Devn* —2D **15**
(nr. Cornwood)
Lutton. *Devn* —1A **16**
(nr. South Brent)
Lutworthy. *Devn* —2B **28**
Luxborough. *Som* —3D **35**
Luxulyan. *Corn* —2C **13**
Lydcott. *Devn* —3A **34**
Lydeard St Lawrence. *Som* —3B **36**
Lydford. *Devn* —2D **21**
Lydmarsh. *Som* —3D **31**
Lyme Regis. *Dors* —1D **25**
Lympsham. *Som* —1D **37**
Lympstone. *Devn* —2D **23**
Lynbridge. *Devn* —2B **34**
Lynch. *Som* —2D **35**
Lyng. *Som* —1D **31**
Lynmouth. *Devn* —2B **34**
Lynstone. *Corn* —3A **26**
Lynton. *Devn* —2B **34**

Mabe Burnthouse. *Corn* —1B **8**
Maddaford. *Devn* —1D **21**
Maders. *Corn* —3B **20**
Madford. *Devn* —2B **30**
Madron. *Corn* —2B **6**
Maenporth. *Corn* —2B **8**
Maer. *Corn* —3A **26**
Maidenwell. *Corn* —3D **19**
Maldencombe. *Devn* —1D **17**
Malmsmead. *Devn* —2B **34**
Malpass. *Corn* —3A **12**
Manaccan. *Corn* —2B **8**
Manaton. *Devn* —2B **22**
Manley. *Devn* —2D **29**
Marazanvose. *Corn* —2D **11**
Marazion. *Corn* —2C **7**
Marhamchurch. *Corn* —3A **26**
Mariansleigh. *Devn* —1B **28**
Mark. *Som* —2D **37**
Mark Causeway. *Som* —2D **37**
Markwell. *Corn* —2B **14**
Marldon. *Devn* —1C **17**
Marsh. *Devn* —2C **31**
Marshalsea. *Dors* —3D **31**
Marsh Barton. *Devn* —1D **23**
Marshgate. *Corn* —1D **19**
Marsh Green. *Devn* —1A **24**
Marsh Street. *Som* —2D **35**
Marshwood. *Dors* —1D **25**
Martinhoe. *Devn* —2A **34**
Martinhoe Cross. *Devn* —2A **34**
Marwood. *Devn* —3D **33**
Marystow. *Devn* —2C **21**
Mary Tavy. *Devn* —3D **21**
Mawgan. *Corn* —2B **8**
Mawla. *Corn* —3D **11**
Mawnan. *Corn* —2B **8**
Mawnan Smith. *Corn* —2B **8**
Maxworthy. *Corn* —1A **20**
Mayfield. *Corn* —2C **15**
Mayon. *Corn* —3A **6**
Maypole. *IOS* —1B **66**
Mead. *Devn* —2A **26**
Meadwell. *Devn* —2C **21**
Meare Green. *Som* —1D **31**
(nr. Stoke St Gregory)
Meare Green. *Som* —1C **31**
(nr. Wrantage)
Meavy. *Devn* —1D **15**
Meddon. *Devn* —2A **26**
Medlyn. *Corn* —1B **8**
Meeth. *Devn* —3D **27**
Melbur. *Corn* —2B **12**
Meldon. *Devn* —1D **21**
Membury. *Devn* —3C **31**
Menagissey. *Corn* —3D **11**
Menerdue. *Corn* —1B **8**
Menheniot. *Corn* —1A **14**
Menherion. *Corn* —1B **8**
Menna. *Corn* —2B **12**
Merridge. *Som* —3C **37**
Merrifield. *Devn* —3A **26**
(nr. Bridgerule)
Merrifield. *Devn* —3C **17**
(nr. Slapton)
Merriott. *Som* —2D **31**
Merrivale. *Devn* —3D **21**
Merrymeet. *Corn* —1A **14**
Merther. *Corn* —3A **12**
Merton. *Devn* —2D **27**
Meshaw. *Devn* —2B **28**
Metcombe. *Devn* —1A **24**
Metherell. *Corn* —1C **15**
Mevagissey. *Corn* —3C **13**
Michaelstow. *Corn* —3C **19**
Michelcombe. *Devn* —1A **16**
Middle Burnham. *Som* —1D **37**
Middlecott. *Devn* —2B **22**
Middlehill. *Corn* —1A **14**
Middle Marwood. *Devn* —3D **33**
Middlemoor. *Devn* —3C **21**
Middle Rocombe. *Devn* —1D **17**
Middle Stoughton. *Som* —2D **37**
Middle Taphouse. *Corn* —1D **13**
Middle Town. *IOS* —1B **66**
Middlewood. *Corn* —3A **20**
Middlezoy. *Som* —3D **37**
Mid Lambrook. *Som* —2D **31**
Mile End. *Devn* —3C **23**
Milford. *Devn* —1A **26**
Millbrook. *Corn* —2C **15**
Millbrook. *Devn* —3B **34**
Millcombe. *Corn* —3B **20**
Millcombe. *Devn* —3C **17**
Millhayes. *Devn* —2B **30**
(nr. Hemyock)
Millhayes. *Devn* —3C **31**
(nr. Stockland)
Millhill. *Devn* —3C **21**
Millook. *Corn* —1D **19**
Millpool. *Corn* —3D **19**
Milltown. *Devn* —3D **33**
Milton. *N Som* —1D **37**
Milton Abbot. *Devn* —3C **21**
Milton Combe. *Devn* —1C **15**
Milton Damerel. *Devn* —2B **26**
Milverton. *Som* —1B **30**
Minehead. *Som* —2D **35**
Mingoose. *Corn* —3D **11**
Minions. *Corn* —3A **20**
Misterton. *Som* —3D **31**
Mitchell. *Corn* —2A **12**
Mithian. *Corn* —2D **11**
Mixtow. *Corn* —2D **13**
Modbury. *Devn* —2A **16**
Mogworthy. *Devn* —2C **29**
Molland. *Devn* —1C **29**
Monkleigh. *Devn* —1C **27**
Monkokehampton. *Devn* —3D **27**
Monksilver. *Som* —3A **36**
Monkton. *Devn* —3B **30**
Monkton Heathfield. *Som* —1C **31**
Monkton Wyld. *Dors* —1D **25**
Moorbath. *Dors* —1D **25**
Moorhayes. *Devn* —2D **29**
Moorland. *Som* —3D **37**
Moorlinch. *Som* —3D **37**
Moorshop. *Devn* —3D **21**
Moorswater. *Corn* —1A **14**
Moortown. *Devn* —3D **21**
Morchard Bishop. *Devn* —3B **28**
Morchard Road. *Devn* —3B **2**
Morcombelake. *Dors* —1D **25**
Morebath. *Devn* —1D **29**
Moreleigh. *Devn* —2B **16**
Moretonhampstead. *Devn* —2B **2**
Mornacott. *Devn* —1B **28**
Mornick. *Corn* —3B **20**
Mortehoe. *Devn* —2C **33**
Morvah. *Corn* —2B **6**
Morval. *Corn* —2A **14**
Morwenstow. *Corn* —2A **26**
Mosterton. *Dors* —3D **31**
Mothecombe. *Devn* —3A **16**
Mount. *Corn* —1D **13**
Mount Ambrose. *Corn* —3D **1**
Mount Hawke. *Corn* —3D **11**
Mountjoy. *Corn* —1A **12**
Mount Pleasant. *Corn* —1C **13**
Mousehole. *Corn* —3B **6**
Muchelney. *Som* —1D **31**
Muchelney Ham. *Som* —1D **3**
Muchlarnick. *Corn* —2A **14**
Muddiford. *Devn* —3D **33**
Muddlebridge. *Devn* —3D **33**
Mudgley. *Som* —2D **37**
Mullacott. *Devn* —2D **33**
Mullacott Cross. *Devn* —2D **3**
Mullion. *Corn* —3A **8**
Mullion Cove. *Corn* —3A **8**
Murchington. *Devn* —2A **22**
Musbury. *Devn* —1C **25**
Mutterton. *Devn* —3A **30**
Mylor Bridge. *Corn* —1C **9**
Mylor Churchtown. *Corn* —1C

Nailsbourne *Som* —1C **31**
Nancledra. *Corn* —2B **6**
Nanpean. *Corn* —2B **12**
Nanstallon. *Corn* —1C **13**
Nantithet. *Corn* —3D **7**
Narcegollan. *Corn* —2D **7**
Narkurs. *Corn* —2B **14**
Natcott. *Devn* —1A **26**
Navarino. *Corn* —2A **20**
Neopardy. *Devn* —1B **22**
Nethercott. *Devn* —1B **20**
Nether Exe. *Devn* —3D **29**
Nether Stowey. *Som* —3B **36**
Netherton. *Corn* —3A **20**
Netherton. *Devn* —3C **23**
Netton. *Devn* —3D **15**
Newbridge. *Corn* —1B **14**
(nr. Callington)
Newbridge. *Corn* —2B **6**
(nr. Madron)
Newbridge. *Corn* —3D **11**
(nr. Truro)
New Buildings. *Devn* —3B **28**
Newbury. *Devn* —1B **22**
Newcott. *Devn* —3C **31**
Newford. *IOS* —1B **66**
New Grimsby. *IOS* —1A **66**
New Inn. *Devn* —3C **27**
Newland. *Som* —3C **35**
New Mill. *Corn* —2B **6**
(nr. Penzance)
New Mill. *Corn* —3A **12**
(nr. Truro)
New Mills. *Corn* —2A **12**
New Polzeath. *Corn* —3B **18**
Newport. *Corn* —2B **20**
Newport. *Devn* —3D **33**
Newport. *Som* —1D **31**
Newquay. *Corn* —1A **12**
Newton. *Som* —3B **36**
Newton Abbot. *Devn* —3C **23**
Newton Ferrers. *Devn* —3D **1**
Newton Poppleford. *Devn* —2A **2**
Newton St Cyres. *Devn* —1C **2**
Newton St Petrock. *Devn* —2C **2**
Newton Tracey. *Devn* —1D **27**
Newtown. *Corn* —3A **20**
New Town. *Devn* —1B **28**
(nr. Bishop's Nympton)
Newtown. *Devn* —1A **24**
(nr. Whimple)
Newtown. *Som* —2C **31**
Newtown-in-St Martin. *Corn* —2B
Nicholashayne. *Devn* —2B **30**
Nightcott. *Som* —1C **29**
Nine Oaks. *Devn* —1A **24**

70 Visitors' Devon & Cornwall Atlas

Salwayash. *Dors* —1D 25
Samford Arundel. *Som* —2B 30
Samford Moor. *Som* —2B 30
Samford Peverell. *Devn* —2A 30
Sampford Brett. *Som* —2A 36
Sampford Chapple. *Devn* —3A 28
Sampford Courtenay. *Devn* —3A 28
Sampford Spiney. *Devn* —3D 21
Sancreed. *Corn* —3B 6
Sand. *Som* —2D 37
Sandford. *Devn* —3C 29
Sandford. *N Som* —1D 37
Sandplace. *Corn* —2A 14
Sandy Park. *Devn* —2B 22
Satterleigh. *Devn* —1A 28
Saunton. *Devn* —3C 33
Scarcewater. *Corn* —2B 12
Scobbiscombe *Devn* —3A 16
Scorrier. *Corn* —3D 11
Scorriton. *Devn* —1B 16
Sea. *Som* —2D 31
Seaborough. *Dors* —3D 31
Seaton. *Corn* —2B 14
Seaton. *Devn* —1C 25
Seaton Junction. *Devn* —1C 25
Seatown. *Dors* —1D 25
Seavington St Mary. *Som* —2D 31
Seavington St Michael. *Som* —2D 31
Selworthy. *Som* —2D 35
Sennen. *Corn* —3A 6
Sennen Cove. *Corn* —3A 6
Seven Ash. *Som* —3B 36
Seworgan. *Corn* —1B 8
Shaldon. *Devn* —3D 23
Shallowford. *Devn* —2B 34 (nr. Lynton)
Shallowford. *Devn* —3A 22 (nr. Pansworthy)
Shapwick. *Som* —3D 37
Shaugh Prior. *Devn* —1D 15
Shearston. *Som* —3C 37
Shebbear. *Devn* —3C 27
Sheepstor. *Devn* —1D 15
Sheepwash. *Devn* —3C 27 (nr. Black Torrington)
Sheepwash. *Devn* —1B 28 (nr. Molland)
Sheffield. *Devn* —3B 6
Sheldon. *Devn* —3B 30
Shepherds. *Corn* —2A 12
Shepton Beauchamp. *Som* —2D 31
Sherford. *Devn* —3B 16
Sherwood Green. *Devn* —1D 27
Sheviock. *Corn* —2B 14
Shillingford. *Devn* —1D 29
Shillingford Abbot. *Devn* —2D 23
Shillingford St George. *Devn* —2D 23
Shinner's Bridge. *Devn* —1B 16
Shipham. *Som* —1D 37
Shiphay. *Devn* —1C 17
Shirwell. *Devn* —3D 33
Shobrooke. *Devn* —3C 29
Shop. *Corn* —3A 18 (nr. Padstow)
Shop. *Corn* —2A 26 (nr. Woodford)
Shop. *Devn* —2B 26
Shore Bottom. *Devn* —3C 31
Shoreditch. *Som* —1C 31
Shortacross. *Corn* —2A 14
Shortlanesend. *Corn* —3A 12
Shurton. *Som* —2C 37
Shute. *Devn* —3C 29 (nr. Crediton)
Shute. *Devn* —1C 25 (nr. Kilmington)
Sid. *Devn* —2B 24
Sidbury. *Devn* —1B 24
Sidcot. *N Som* —1D 37
Sidford. *Devn* —1B 24
Sidmouth. *Devn* —2B 24
Sigford. *Devn* —3B 22
Silford. *Devn* —1C 27
Sillaton. *Corn* —1B 14
Silverton. *Devn* —3D 29
Silverwell. *Corn* —3D 11
Simonsbath. *Som* —3B 34
Sithney. *Corn* —3D 7

Sithney Green. *Corn* —3D 7
Skillgate. *Som* —1D 29
Skinner's Bottom. *Corn* —3D 11
Sladesbridge. *Corn* —3C 19
Slape Cross. *Som* —3D 37
Slapton. *Devn* —3C 17
Slipperhill. *Corn* —3A 20
Sloncombe. *Devn* —2B 22
Slough Green. *Som* —2C 31
Smallbrook. *Devn* —1C 23
Smallridge. *Devn* —3D 31
Smeatharpe. *Devn* —2B 30
Smithincott. *Devn* —2A 30
Snapper. *Devn* —3D 33
Soldon Cross. *Devn* —2B 26
Sourton. *Devn* —1D 21
South Bowood. *Dors* —1D 25
South Brent. *Devn* —1A 16
South Carne. *Corn* —2A 20
South Chard. *Som* —3D 31
Southcott. *Devn* —2C 27
Southdown. *Corn* —2C 15
Southerton. *Devn* —1A 24
South Hill. *Corn* —3B 20
South Hole. *Devn* —1A 26
South Knighton. *Devn* —3C 23
Southleigh. *Devn* —1C 25
South Milton. *Devn* —3A 16
South Molton. *Devn* —1B 28
South Petherton. *Som* —2D 31
South Petherwin. *Corn* —2B 20
South Pool. *Devn* —3B 16
South Radworthy. *Devn* —3B 34
South Tawton. *Devn* —1A 22
South Tehidy. *Corn* —1D 7
South Wheatley. *Corn* —1A 20
South Zeal. *Devn* —1A 22
Sowton. *Devn* —1D 23
Sparkwell. *Devn* —2D 15
Sparnon Gate. *Corn* —1D 7
Spaxton. *Devn* —3C 37
Splatt. *Corn* —3B 18 (nr. Padstow)
Splatt. *Corn* —2A 20 (nr. Warbstow)
Spreyton. *Devn* —1A 22
Spriddlestone. *Devn* —2D 15
Staddiscombe. *Plym* —2D 15
Staddon. *Devn* —3B 26
Stafford Barton. *Devn* —3B 30
Stag's Head. *Devn* —1A 28
Staple Cross. *Devn* —1A 30
Staple Fitzpaine. *Som* —2C 31
Staplegrove. *Som* —1C 31
Staplehay. *Som* —1C 31
Stapley. *Som* —2B 30
Starcross. *Devn* —2D 23
Start. *Devn* —3C 17
Stathe. *Som* —1D 31
Staverton. *Devn* —1B 16
Stawell. *Som* —3D 37
Stawley. *Som* —1A 30
Steart. *Som* —2C 37
Stembridge. *Som* —1D 31
Stenalees. *Corn* —2C 13
Stenhill. *Devn* —2A 30
Stewley. *Som* —2D 31
Stibb. *Corn* —2A 26
Stibb Cross. *Devn* —2C 27
Sticker. *Corn* —2B 12
Sticklepath. *Devn* —3D 33 (nr. Barnstaple)
Sticklepath. *Devn* —1A 22 (nr. South Zeal)
Stithians. *Corn* —1B 8
Stockland. *Devn* —3C 31
Stockland Bristol. *Som* —2C 37
Stockleigh English. *Devn* —3C 29
Stockleigh Pomeroy. *Devn* —3C 29
Stocklinch. *Som* —2D 31
Stockwell. *Devn* —3D 29
Stogumber. *Som* —3A 36
Stogursey. *Som* —2C 37
Stoke. *Devn* —1A 26
Stoke. *Plym* —2C 15
Stoke Abbott. *Dors* —3D 31
Stoke Canon. *Devn* —1D 23
Stoke Climsland. *Corn* —3B 20
Stoke Fleming. *Devn* —3C 17
Stoke Gabriel. *Devn* —2C 17
Stokeinteignhead. *Devn* —3D 23
Stokenham. *Devn* —3C 17

Stoke Pero. *Som* —2C 35
Stoke Rivers. *Devn* —3A 34
Stoke St Gregory. *Som* —1D 31
Stoke St Mary. *Som* —1C 31
Stolford. *Som* —2C 37
Stone Allerton. *Som* —1D 37
Stonebridge. *N Som* —1D 37
Stoneyford. *Devn* —3A 30 (nr. Cullompton)
Stoneyford. *Devn* —2A 24 (nr. Newton Poppleford)
Stony Cross. *Devn* —1D 27
Stoodleigh. *Devn* —2D 29 (nr. Cove)
Stoodleigh. *Devn* —3A 34 (nr. West Buckland)
Stoodleigh Barton. *Devn* —3A 34
Stoptide. *Corn* —3B 18
Stowford. *Devn* —1A 28 (nr. Chittlehampton)
Stowford. *Devn* —2A 24 (nr. Colaton Raleigh)
Stowford. *Devn* —1C 21 (nr. Halwill Junction)
Stowford. *Devn* —2C 21 (nr. Portgate)
Stowford. *Devn* —2B 24 (nr. Sidmouth)
Stratton. *Corn* —3A 26
Stream. *Som* —3A 36
Street. *Corn* —1A 20
Street. *Devn* —2B 24
Street. *Som* —3D 31
Stretch Down. *Devn* —2C 29
Stretcholt. *Som* —2C 37
Strete. *Devn* —3C 17
Strete Raleigh. *Devn* —1A 24
Stringston. *Som* —2B 36
Summercourt. *Corn* —2A 12
Sutcombe. *Devn* —2B 26
Sutcombe Mill. *Devn* —2B 26
Sutton. *Devn* —3A 20
Sutton. *Devn* —3B 16
Sutton Mallet. *Som* —3D 37
Sweetham. *Devn* —1C 23
Sweethouse. *Corn* —1C 13
Sweets. *Corn* —1D 19
Swell. *Som* —1D 31
Swimbridge. *Devn* —1A 28
Swimbridge Newland. *Devn* —3A 34
Sydenham. *Som* —3D 37
Sydenham Damerel *Devn* —3C 21
Symondsbury. *Dors* —1D 25

Taddiport. *Devn* —2C 27
Talaton. *Devn* —1A 24
Taleford. *Devn* —1A 24
Talskiddy. *Corn* —1B 12
Tamerton Foliot. *Plym* —1C 15
Tarnock. *Som* —1D 37
Tarr. *Som* —3B 36
Taunton. *Som* —1C 31
Tavistock. *Devn* —3C 21
Taw Green. *Devn* —1A 22
Tawstock. *Devn* —1D 27
Tedburn St Mary. *Devn* —1C 23
Teigncombe. *Devn* —2A 22
Teign Village. *Devn* —2C 23
Telngrace. *Devn* —3C 23
Temple. *Corn* —3D 19
Templeton. *Devn* —2C 29
Terras. *Corn* —2B 12
Tetcott. *Devn* —1B 20
Thelbridge Barton. *Devn* —2B 28
Thornbury. *Devn* —3C 27
Thorne St Margaret. *Som* —1A 30
Thorncombe. *Dors* —3D 31
Thorncroft. *Devn* —1B 16
Thorndon Cross. *Devn* —1D 21
Thorne. *Corn* —3A 26 (nr. Bude)
Thorne. *Devn* —2A 26 (nr. Kilkhampton)
Thornehillhead. *Devn* —2C 27
Thorne Moor. *Devn* —2B 20
Thorney. *Som* —1D 31
Thornfalcon. *Som* —1C 31
Thorngrove. *Som* —3D 37
Thorverton. *Devn* —3D 29
Three Burrows. *Corn* —3D 11

Three Hammers. *Corn* —2A 20
Threemilestone. *Corn* —3D 11
Three Oaks. *Devn* —3C 21
Throwleigh. *Devn* —1A 22
Thrushelton. *Devn* —2C 21
Thurdon. *Corn* —2A 26
Thurlestone. *Devn* —3A 16
Thurloxton. *Som* —3C 37
Tideford. *Corn* —2B 14
Tideford Cross. *Corn* —1B 14
Tigley. *Devn* —1B 16
Tilland. *Devn* —1B 14
Timberscombe. *Som* —2D 35
Tinhay. *Devn* —2B 20
Tintagel. *Corn* —1C 19
Tippacott. *Devn* —2B 34
Tipton St John. *Devn* —1A 24
Titchberry. *Devn* —1A 26
Titson. *Corn* —3A 26
Tiverton. *Devn* —2D 29
Tivington. *Som* —2D 35
Toldish. *Corn* —2B 12
Tolland. *Som* —3B 36
Topsham. *Devn* —2D 23
Tor. *Devn* —2D 15
Torbryan. *Devn* —1C 17
Torfrey. *Corn* —2D 13
Torpoint. *Corn* —2C 15
Tor Royal. *Devn* —3D 21
Totnes. *Devn* —1B 16
Toulton. *Som* —3B 36
Towan. *Corn* —3A 18
Towan Cross. *Corn* —3D 11
Towans, The. *Corn* —2C 7
Towednack. *Corn* —2B 6
Townshend. *Corn* —2C 7
Town, The. *IOS* —1A 66
Traboe. *Corn* —2B 8
Tracebridge. *Devn* —1A 30
Treamble. *Corn* —2D 11
Treator. *Corn* —3B 18
Trebartha. *Corn* —3A 20
Trebarwith. *Corn* —2C 19
Trebeath. *Corn* —2A 20
Trebehor. *Corn* —3A 6
Trebetherick. *Corn* —3B 18
Treborough. *Som* —3A 36
Trebudannon. *Corn* —1A 12
Trebullett. *Corn* —3B 20
Treburley. *Corn* —3B 20
Treburrick. *Corn* —3A 18
Trebyan. *Corn* —1C 13
Trecott. *Devn* —3A 28
Trecrogo. *Corn* —2B 20
Tredaule. *Corn* —2A 20
Tredinnick. *Corn* —2A 14 (nr. Duloe)
Tredinnick. *Corn* —3B 18 (nr. St Issey)
Tredinnick. *Corn* —1D 13 (nr. St Neot)
Tredrizzick. *Corn* —3B 18
Treen. *Corn* —2B 6 (nr. Porthmeor)
Treen. *Corn* —3A 6 (nr. St Buryan)
Tregadillet. *Corn* —2A 20
Tregamere. *Corn* —1B 12
Tregargus. *Corn* —2B 12
Tregarland. *Corn* —2A 14
Tregarne. *Corn* —2B 8
Tregarrick Mill. *Corn* —2A 14
Tregaswith. *Corn* —1A 12
Tregatillian. *Corn* —1B 12
Tregatta. *Corn* —1C 19
Tregavarras. *Corn* —3B 12
Tregda. *Corn* —2B 20
Tregear. *Corn* —2A 12
Tregeare. *Corn* —2A 20
Tregerrick. *Corn* —3B 12
Tregeseal. *Corn* —2A 6
Tregiskey. *Corn* —3C 13
Tregole. *Corn* —1D 19
Tregonce. *Corn* —3B 18
Tregonetha. *Corn* —1B 12
Tregonhawke. *Corn* —2C 15
Tregony. *Corn* —3B 12
Tregoodwell. *Corn* —2C 19
Tregorrick. *Corn* —2C 13
Tregoss. *Corn* —1B 12
Tregowris. *Corn* —2B 8
Tregrehan Mills. *Corn* —2C 13
Tregullon. *Corn* —1C 13
Tregunna. *Corn* —3B 18
Tregunnon. *Corn* —2A 20
Tregurrian. *Corn* —1A 12

Trehan. *Corn* —2C 15
Trehunist. *Corn* —1B 14
Trekelland. *Corn* —3A 20 (nr. South Petherwin)
Trekelland. *Corn* —2B 20 (nr. Tregda)
Trekenner. *Corn* —3B 20
Trekenning. *Corn* —1B 12
Treknow. *Corn* —2C 19
Trelan. *Corn* —3B 8
Trelash. *Corn* —1D 19
Trelassick. *Corn* —2A 12
Treleaver. *Corn* —3B 8
Trelew. *Corn* —1C 9
Treligga. *Corn* —2C 19
Trelights. *Corn* —3B 18
Trelill. *Corn* —3C 19
Trelion. *Corn* —2B 12
Trelissick. *Corn* —1C 9
Trelow. *Corn* —1B 12
Trelowia. *Corn* —2A 14
Trelowth. *Corn* —2B 12
Trelowthas. *Corn* —3A 12
Treluggan. *Corn* —1C 9
Tremail. *Corn* —2D 19
Tremaine. *Corn* —2A 20
Tremar. *Corn* —1A 14
Trematon. *Corn* —2B 14
Trembraze. *Corn* —1A 14
Tremollett. *Corn* —3A 20
Tremore. *Corn* —1C 13
Trenance. *Corn* —3B 18 (nr. St Issey)
Trenance. *Corn* —1A 12 (nr. St Mawgan)
Trenant. *Corn* —1A 14
Trenarren. *Corn* —3C 13
Trencreek. *Corn* —1A 12
Trendeal. *Corn* —2A 12
Trendrossel. *Corn* —2B 14
Treneague. *Corn* —3B 18
Trenear. *Corn* —2D 7
Treneglos. *Corn* —2A 20
Trenewan. *Corn* —2D 13
Trengune. *Corn* —1D 19
Trenode. *Corn* —2A 14
Trenoweth. *Corn* —1B 8
Trenoweth. *IOS* —1B 66
Trentishoe. *Devn* —2A 34
Trenwheal. *Corn* —2D 7
Trequite. *Corn* —3C 19
Trerulefoot. *Corn* —2B 14
Tresawle. *Corn* —3A 12
Tresawsen. *Corn* —3D 11
Trescowe. *Corn* —2C 7
Tresean. *Corn* —2D 11
Tresevern Croft. *Corn* —1B 8
Tresillian. *Corn* —3A 12
Treskillard. *Corn* —2D 7
Treskinnick Cross. *Corn* —1A 20
Treslea. *Corn* —1D 13
Treslothan. *Corn* —2D 7
Tresmeer. *Corn* —2A 20
Tresowes Green. *Corn* —3C 7
Tresparrett. *Corn* —1D 19
Tresparrett Posts. *Corn* —1D 1.
Trespearne. *Corn* —2A 20
Trethevey. *Corn* —2C 19
Trethewey. *Corn* —3A 6
Trethosa. *Corn* —2B 12
Trethurgy. *Corn* —2C 13
Trevadlock. *Corn* —3A 20
Trevalga. *Corn* —1C 19
Trevance. *Corn* —3B 18
Trevanger. *Corn* —3B 18
Trevanson. *Corn* —3B 18
Trevarnon. *Corn* —3A 18
Trevarrack. *Corn* —2B 6
Trevarren. *Corn* —1B 12
Trevarrian. *Corn* —1A 12
Trevarrick. *Corn* —3B 12
Trevarth. *Corn* —3D 11
Trevaylor. *Corn* —2B 6
Treveal. *Corn* —2D 11
Treveighan. *Corn* —3C 19
Trevellas. *Corn* —2D 11
Trevelmond. *Corn* —1A 14
Trevemper. *Corn* —2A 12
Treveor. *Corn* —3B 12
Treverbyn. *Corn* —2C 13 (nr. St Austell)
Treverbyn. *Corn* —1A 14 (nr. St Neot)
Treverva. *Corn* —1B 8
Trevescan. *Corn* —3A 6

HOW TO USE THE PLACES OF INTEREST INDEX

Places of interest are represented by the appropriate symbol on the map together with red text in a yellow box. The index reference is to the square in which symbol (or its pointer) appears, not to the text box; e.g. Bampton —1D **29** is to be found in square 1D on page **29**. The page number being shown in bold ty

Entries shown without an index reference have the name of the appropriate town plan on which they appear. For reasons of clarity, these places of interest do appear on the main map pages. The extent of these town plans are indicated on the main pages by a blue box.

Terms such as 'museum', 'country park' etc. are omitted from the text on the map.

Entries in italics are not named on the map but are shown with a symbol.
Entries in italics and enclosed in brackets are not shown on the map.
For both these types of entry, the nearest village or town name is given, where that name is not already included in the name of the place of interest.

Opening times for places of interest vary considerably depending on the season, day of week or the ownership of the property. Please check with the nearest tourist information centre listed below before starting your journey.

Tourist Information Centre (Open All Year)

Bampton — 1D **29**
Barnstaple, Tel: 01271 375000
Bideford — 1C **27**, Tel: 01237 477676 / 421853
Bodmin, Tel: 01208 76616
Boscastle — 1D **19**, Tel: 01840 250010
Braunton — 3C **33**, Tel: 01271 816400
Brixham, Tel: 01803 852861
Bude, Tel: 01288 354240
Budleigh Salterton — 2A **24**, Tel: 01395 445275
Burnham-on-Sea — 2D **37**, Tel: 01278 787852
Chard — 3D **31**, Tel: 01460 67463
Dartmouth, Tel: 01803 834224
Dawlish — 3D **23**, Tel: 01626 863589
Exeter Services, M5, junction 30 — 1D **23**,
    Tel: 01392 437581
Exeter, Tel: 01392 265700
Exmouth — 2A **24**, Tel: 01395 222299
Falmouth, Tel: 01326 312300
Fowey, Tel: 01726 833616
Great Torrington — 2C **27**, Tel: 01805 623302
Helston & Lizard Peninsula — 3D **7**,
    Tel: 01326 565431
Holsworthy — 3B **26**, Tel: 01409 254185
Honiton — 3B **30**, Tel: 01404 43716
Ilfracombe, Tel: 01271 863001
Isles of Scilly, Hugh Town, St Mary's, Isles of Scilly
    — 1B **66**, Tel: 01720 422536
Ivybridge — 2A **16**, Tel: 01752 897035
Kingsbridge — 3B **16**, Tel: 01548 853195
Launceston, Tel: 01566 772321 / 772333
Lostwithiel — 2D **13**, Tel: 01208 872207
Lyme Regis — 1D **25**, Tel: 01297 442138
Lynton, Tel: 01598 752225
Mevagissey — 3C **13**, Tel: 01726 842266
Minehead, Tel: 01643 702624
Newquay, Tel: 01637 871345
Newton Abbot, Tel: 01626 367494
Padstow, Tel: 01841 533449
Paignton, Tel: 01803 558383
Penzance, Tel: 01736 362207
Perranporth — 2D **11**, Tel: 01872 573368
Plymouth Discovery Centre, Crabtree, Plymouth
    — 2D **15**, Tel: 01752 266030 / 266031
Plymouth, Tel: 01752 264849
St Ives, Tel: 01736 796297
Salcombe — 3B **16**, Tel: 01548 843927
Seaton — 2C **25**, Tel: 01297 21660 / 21689
Sedgemoor Services (Somerset Visitor Centre), M5
    South, East Brent — 1D **37**, Tel: 01934 750833
Sidmouth — 2B **24**, Tel: 01395 516441
Taunton, Tel: 01823 336344
Tavistock — 3C **21**, Tel: 01822 612938
Teignmouth — 3D **23**, Tel: 01626 779769
Tiverton — 2D **29**, Tel: 01884 255827
Torquay, Tel: 01803 297428
Totnes — 1C **17**, Tel: 01803 863168
Truro, Tel: 01872 274555
Wadebridge — 3B **18**, Tel: 01208 813725
Weston-super-Mare — 1D **37**, Tel: 01934 888800

Tourist Information Centre (Summer Season Only)

Ashburton Community Information Point
    — 1B **16**, Tel: 01364 653426

Axminster — 1C **25**, Tel: 01297 34386
Bovey Tracey — 3C **23**, Tel: 01626 832047
Bridgwater — 3C **37**, Tel: 01278 427652
Camelford — 2D **19**, Tel: 01840 212954
Combe Martin — 2D **33**, Tel: 01271 883319
Crediton — 3C **29**, Tel: 01363 772006
Crewkerne — 3D **31**, Tel: 01460 73441
Hayle — 2C **7**, Tel: 01736 754399
Ilminster — 2D **31**, Tel: 01460 57294
Langport — 1D **31**, Tel: 01458 253527
Looe, Tel: 01503 262072
Modbury — 2A **16**, Tel: 01548 830159
Okehampton — 1D **21**, Tel: 01837 53020
Ottery St Mary — 1A **24**, Tel: 01404 813964
Polzeath — 3B **18**, Tel: 01208 862488
Porlock — 2C **35**, Tel: 01643 863150
St Austell — 2C **13**, Tel: 01726 76333
Shaldon Tourist Centre — 3D **23**,
    Tel: 01626 873723
South Molton — 1B **28**, Tel: 01769 574122
Tiverton Services, M5, junction 27 — 2A **30**,
    Tel: 01884 821242
Watchet Tourism Office — 2A **36**
Wellington — 1B **30**, Tel: 01823 664747
Woolacombe — 2C **33**, Tel: 01271 870553

Visitor Centre/Information Centre (National Park)

Combe Martin Visitor Centre NP — 2D **33**,
    Tel: 01271 883319
County Gate Visitor Centre NP — 2B **34**,
    Tel: 01598 741321
Dulverton Visitor Centre NP — 1D **29**,
    Tel: 01398 323841
Dunster Visitor Centre NP — 2D **35**,
    Tel: 01643 821835
Haytor Information Centre, Haytor Vale NP
    — 3B **22**, Tel: 01364 661520
High Moorland Visitor Centre, Princetown NP
    — 3D **21**, Tel: 01822 890414
Lynmouth Visitor Centre NP — Lynton & Lynmouth,
    Tel: 01598 752509
Moretonhampstead Visitor Information Centre NP
    — 2B **22**, Tel: 01647 440043
Newbridge Information Centre, Poundsgate NP
    — 3B **22**, Tel: 01364 631303
Postbridge Information Centre NP — 3A **22**,
    Tel: 01822 880272

Visitor Centre/Information Centre (National Trust)

Boscastle Old Forge Information Centre NT
    — 1C **19**, Tel: 01840 250353
Carnewas (Bedruthan Steps) Information Centre,
    Trenance NT — 1A **12**, Tel: 01637 860563
Heddon Valley Shop Information Centre, Martinhoe
    NT — 2A **34**, Tel: 01598 763402
Plymouth Elizabethan House Information Centre NT
    — Plymouth, Tel: 01752 253871
Selworthy Information Centre NT — 2D **35**
Sexton's Cottage Information Centre, Widecombe in
    the Moor NT — 3B **22**
Trevigue Farm Information Centre NT — 1D **19**,
    Tel: 01840 230418

Watersmeet House Information Centre NT — 2
    Tel: 01598 753348

Abbey/Friary/Priory

See also Cathedral, Church

Berry Tower — Bodmin
Buckfast Abbey — 1B **16**
Cleeve Abbey EH — 2A **36**
Dunkeswell Abbey — 2B **30**
Exeter St Nicholas Priory — Exeter
Frithelstock Priory — 2C **27**
Launceston St Thomas's Priory — Launceston
Muchelney Abbey EH — 1D **31**
Tavistock Abbey — 3C **21**

Animal Collection

See also Farm Park, Wildlife Park, Zoo

Animal Tracks — 1B **28**
Bee World & Animal Centre — 3B **36**
Bolberry Donkey Stud — 3A **16**
Cornwall Donkey & Pony Sanctuary, The — 3C
Dartmoor Otter Sanctuary — 1B **16**
Donkey Sanctuary, The — 2B **24**
Escot Park & Gardens — 1A **24**
Ferne Animal Sanctuary — 3C **31**
Heaven's Gate Farm (Somerset Animal Rescue
    Centre) — 3D **37**
Miniature Pony Centre, The — 2B **22**
Monkey Sanctuary, The — 2A **14**
Mullacott Miniature Ponies & Shire Horse Centr
    — 2D **33**
National Seal Sanctuary — 2B **8**
National Shire Horse Centre, The — 2D **15**
Shaldon Wildlife Trust — 3D **23**
Tamar Otter Sanctuary, The — 2A **20**
Widewalls Animal Sanctuary —2D **19**

Aquarium

Aqualand — Torquay
Brixham Aquarium — Brixham
Fowey Aquarium — Fowey
Living from the Sea Aquarium — Looe
Lyme Regis Marine Aquarium (& Cobb History)
    — 1D **25**
Mevagissey Harbour Marine Aquarium — 3C **13**
National Marine Aquarium — Plymouth
Newquay Sea Life Aquarium — Newquay
Weston-super-Mare Sea Life Aquarium — 1D **3**

Arboretum/Botanical Garden

See also Garden

Burrator Reservoir Arboretum — 1D **15**
Eden Project, The — 2C **13**

Blackdown Hills Welcome Centre — 2B **30**
Blagdon Farm — 1B **20**
Bossington Farm & Birds of Prey Centre — 2C **35**
Cheese Farm, The (Lynher Dairies) — 3A **20**
Churchill Farm — 3B **16**
Court Farm Country Park — 1D **37**
Crealy — 1A **24**
Dairyland Farm World — 2A **12**
East Lydeard Country Farm — 1B **30**
Farway Countryside Park — 1B **24**
Fernley's — 3D **19**
Hedgehog Hospital at Prickly Ball Farm — 1C **17**
Home Farm — 2A **36**
North Devon Farm Park — 3A **34**
Old Macdonald's Farm — 3A **18**
Pennywell Farm — 1B **16**
Roskilly's — 2B **8**
Secret World (Badger & Wildlife Rescue Centre)
— 2D **37**
Shire Horse Farm, The — 2D **7**
Sorley Tunnel Adventure Farm — 3B **16**
Tamar Valley Donkey Park, The — 3C **21**
Tordown Farm — 3A **34**
Trenouth Farm Rare Breeds Centre — 3B **18**
Trethorne Leisure Farm — 2A **20**
World of Country Life, The — 2A **24**

Forest Park/National Park

Dartmoor National Park — 3A **22**
Exmoor National Park — 2B **34**

Forest Walk/Nature Trail

See also Nature Reserve

Abbeyford Woods Forest Walks — 1D **21**
Aisholt Ring Walk — 3B **36**
Argal & College Reservoirs Walks — 1B **8**
Arlington Court Nature Walk *NT* — 2A **34**
Ashclyst Forest Walks — 1A **24**
Aylesbeare Common Nature Trail — 2A **24**
Becky Falls Nature Trails — 3B **22**
Bellever Forest Forest Walks — 3A **22**
*Berry Head Country Park Nature Trail, Brixham
— 2D 17*
Bincombe Beeches Nature Trail — 2D **31**
Blagdon Farm Nature Trail — 1B **20**
Bolberry Down Nature Trail *NT* — 3A **16**
Bullers Hill Forest Walks, Kennford — 2C 23
Bullers Hill Forest Walks — 2C **23**
Burrator Reservoir Woodland Walks — 1D **15**
Burridge Woodland Trail, Dulverton — 1D 29
Cann Wood Forest Walk — 2C **15**
Canonteign Falls Nature Trails — 2C **23**
Cardinham Woods Forest Walks — 1C **13**
Cardinham Woods Forest Walks — 1D **13**
Castle Neroche Nature Trail — 2C **31**
Chapel Porth Nature Trail — 1D **7**
Chapel Wood Nature Trails — 2C **33**
Chard Reservoir Walk — 3D **31**
Clatworthy Reservoir Nature Trail — 3A **36**
Cloutsham Woodland Trail *NT* — 2D **35**
Colliford Lake Walks — 3D **19**
Combe Sydenham Country Park Woodland Walks
— 3A **36**
Cookworthy Moor Plantation Forest Walk — 3C **27**
Coombe Valley Nature Trail — 2A **26**
*Cotehele Woodland Walks, St Dominick NT
— 1C 15*
Cothelstone Hill Trail — 3B **36**
Dead Woman's Ditch Trail — 3B **36**
Decoy Country Park Woodland Walks — 3C **23**
Deerpark Forest Forest Trail — 1D **13**
Denham Forest Walk — 1C **15**
East Hill Woodland Walk — 1B **24**
Fernworthy Forest Walks — 2A **22**
Five Pond Wood Trail — 1C **31**
Fyne Court Nature Trails — 3C **37**
Gaff & Undertown Woodland Walk — 1C **13**
Glenthorne Estate Walks, Countisbury — 2B 34
Great Wood Walk — 3B **36**
Hall Walk *NT* — Fowey
Halsdon Nature Trails — 2D **27**

Heddon Valley Nature Walk *NT* — 2A **34**
Hembury Nature Trail, Buckfast NT — 1B 16
Herne Hill Nature Trail — 2D **31**
Herodsfoot Woods Forest Trails — 2A **14**
Heywood Forest Walk — 2A **28**
*Higher Moors Nature Trail, St Mary's, Isles of Scilly
— 1B 66*
Hilltown Wood Forest Walks — 2A **28**
Hinkley Point Nature Trail — 2C **37**
Holsworthy Woods Forest Walk — 3B **26**
Horner Wood Woodland Walks *NT* — 2C **35**
Hurscombe Nature Trail — 3D **35**
Idless Wood Forest Walks — 3A **12**
Kelly Bray Forest Trail — 3B 20
Kilminorth Woods Forest Walks — 2A **14**
Kit Hill Walk — 3B **20**
*Kitley Caves Country Park Woodland Trail,
Yealmpton — 2D 15*
Lanhydrock Nature Walks, Cutmadoc NT — 1C 13
*Longtimber & Pithill Woods Woodland Walks,
Ivybridge — 2A 16*
*Lower Moors Nature Trail, Old Town, St Mary's,
Isles of Scilly — 1B 66*
Lydford Forest Trail — 2C **21**
Mamhead Forest Walk — 2D **23**
Mellingey Mill Woodland Walk — 3B **18**
North Hill Woodland Trail — 2D **35**
Nutcombe Bottom Forest Trails — 2D **35**
Otterhead Lakes Nature Trail — 2C **31**
Pendarves Wood Nature Trail — 2D **7**
Penrose Estate (Loe Pool Nature) Walks *NT* — 3D **7**
Plym Bridge Riverside & Woodland Walks *NT*
— 2D **15**
Quantock Forest Trail — 3B **36**
Red & Southern Red Moors Nature Trail — 1C **13**
Restormel Woodland Trail, Lostwithiel — 1D 13
River Dart Country Park Nature & Tree Trails
— 3B **22**
Roadford Lake Walks — 1C **21**
St Anthony-in-Roseland Nature Walk *NT* — 1C **9**
Salcombe Hill Nature Trail — 2B **24**
Siblyback Lake Walks, St Cleer — 3A 20
Simpson Farm Nature Trail — 3B **26**
Slapton Ley Nature Trail — 3C 17
Staple Plain Trails *NT* — 2B **36**
Steps Bridge Nature Trail *NT* — 2C **23**
Stoke Woods Forest Walks — 1D **23**
Strete Gate Nature Trail — 3C **17**
Swell Wood Woodland Trail — 1D **31**
Tamar Lakes Nature Trail — 2A **26**
Tamar Valley Nature Trails — 1C **15**
*Tehidy Country Park Woodland Trails, Portreath
— 1D 7*
Teign Gorge Walk *NT* — 1B **22**
Thorne Farm Nature Trail — 3B **26**
Town Tree Nature Trail — 1D **31**
Tregassick Nature Walk *NT* — 1C **9**
Tregellast Barton Nature Trails — 2B **8**
Trelissick Woodland Walk NT — 1C 9
Trelowarren Woodland Walk, Garras — 2B 8
*Trenchford & Tottiford Reservoir Walks, Lustleigh
— 2C 23*
Treworgie Barton Woodland Trails — 1D **19**
Weston Woods Nature Trail — 1D **37**
*Wistlandpound Reservoir Nature Trail,
Blackmoor Gate — 2A 34*
Yarner Wood Nature Trails — 3B **22**

Fortress

See also Castle, Castle & Garden

Bayard's Cove Fort *EH* — Dartmouth
Berry Head Fortifications, Brixham — 2D 17
Brean Down Fort — 1C **37**
Chudleigh Fort — 1C **27**
(Crab Quay Battery, Falmouth — 1C 9)
Crownhill Fort — 2C **15**
Fort Charles, Salcombe — 3B 16
Fowey Blockhouse — Fowey
Garrison Walls *EH* — 2A **66**
*Harry's Walls, Hugh Town, St Mary's, Isles of Scilly
EH — 1B 66*
(Little Dennis Blockhouse, Falmouth — 1C 9)
Old Blockhouse, Tresco, Isles of Scilly EH — 1A 66
Plymouth Breakwater Fort — 2C 15

Polruan Blockhouse — Fowey
Royal Citadel, The *EH* — Plymouth
St Anthony Battery NT — 1C 9

Garden

See also Arboretum, Historic Building & Garde

Antony Woodland Garden — 2C **15**
Ashford Gardens — 3D **33**
Avenue Cottage Gardens — 2C **17**
Bickham Barton Gardens — 1C **15**
Bicton College Garden & Arboretum — 2A **24**
Bicton Park & Pleasure Gardens — 2A **24**
Bosvigo Garden — Truro
Burncoose Nurseries Garden — 1B **8**
Burrow Farm Gardens — 1C **25**
Cannington College Heritage Gardens — 3C **37**
Carreg Dhu Gardens — 1B 66
Carwinion Garden — 2B **8**
Catchfrench Manor Gardens — 2B **14**
Clapton Court Gardens — 3D **31**
Cockington Court Gardens — 1C **17**
Coleton Fishacre Garden *NT* — 2D **17**
Cothay Manor Garden — 1A **30**
Creed House Garden — 3B **12**
Dartington Hall Gardens — 1B **16**
Docton Mill Gardens — 1A **26**
Downes Garden, The — 1C **27**
East Lambrook Manor Garden — 2D **31**
Elworthy Cottage Gardens — 3A **36**
Endsleigh House Gardens — 3B **20**
Garden House, The — 1C **15**
Gate House Gardens, The — 2C **33**
Glendurgan Garden *NT* — 2B **8**
Greencombe Garden, West Porlock — 2C 35
Gyllyngdune Gardens — Falmouth
Headland Garden — Fowey
Hestercombe Formal & Landscape Gardens —
Hill House Gardens — 1B **16**
Japanese Garden, The — 1A **12**
Kelways Cottage Gardens — 1D **31**
Ken-Caro Garden — 1B **14**
Kentsford House Gardens — 2A **36**
Lamorran House Garden, St Mawes — 1C 9
Lanterns Garden — 1C **9**
Little Upcott Gardens — 1A **24**
Longcross Victorian Gardens — 3B **18**
Lost Gardens of Heligan, The — 3B **12**
Lower Severalls Garden — 2D **31**
Lukesland Gardens — 2A **16**
Marshford Organic Nursery Garden — 1C **27**
Marwood Hill Gardens — 3D **33**
Maunsel House Gardens — 3D **37**
*Mount Edgcumbe Country Park Formal Garden
Cremyll — 2C 15*
Old Mill Herbary, The — 3C **19**
Overbeck's Garden *NT* — 3B **16**
Penjerrick Gardens — 1B **8**
Pine Lodge Gardens, St Austell — 2C 13
Plant World — 1C **17**
Pleasant View Nursery Garden — 1C **17**
Probus Gardens — 3B **12**
Rock Gardens, The — 3C **23**
Rosemoor Garden (The Royal Horticultural Soc
— 2C **27**
Tapeley Park Gardens — 1C **27**
Tehidy Country Park Rose Garden — 1D **7**
Towan Nurseries Camellia Garden — 1C **9**
Trebah Garden — 2B **8**
Tregrehan — 2C **13**
Trelissick Garden *NT* — 1C **9**
Tremeer Gardens — 3C **19**
Trenance Gardens — Newquay
Trengwainton Garden *NT* — 2B **6**
Tresco Abbey Gardens — 1A **66**
Trevarno Estate & Gardens — 2D **7**
Wetherham Gardens — 3C **19**
Woodland Garden — 2B **8**

Hill Fort

See also Prehistoric Monument

Bat's Castle — 2D **35**

Kents Cavern — 1D **17**
Kitley Caves — 2D **15**
Piper's Hole — 1A **66**
Poldark Mine — 2D **7**
Rosevale Mine — 2A **6**
Vitifer Tin Mine — 2A **22**

Halangy Down Ancient Village, St Mary's, Isles of Scilly *EH* — 1B **66**
Halliggye Fogou *EH* — 2B **8**
Hall Rings — 2A **14**
Hamel Down Barrows — 3B **22**
Hurlers Stone Circles, The *EH* — 3A **20**
Innisidgen Lower & Upper Burial Chambers *EH* — 1B **66**
Joaney How & Robin How Burial Cairns — 2D **35**
Kestor Settlement — 2A **22**
King Arthur's Hall — 3D **19**
Lanyon Quoit *NT* — 2B **6**
Longstone — 2B **34**
Magi Stone — 1B **12**
Meare Lake Villages (site of) — 2D **37**
Men-an-Tol — 2B **6**
Men Scryfa Inscribed Stone — 2B **6**
Merrivale Prehistoric Settlement *EH* — 3D **21**
Merry Maidens Stone Circle — 3B **6**
Mulfra Quoit — 2B **6**
Nine Maidens Stone Circle — 2B **6**
Nine Maidens Stone Row — 1B **12**
Old Man of Gugh, Gugh, Isles of Scilly — 2A **66**
Pawton Quoit — 1B **12**
Pipers Standing Stones, The — 3B **6**
Porlock Stone Circle — 2C **35**
Porth Hellick Down Burial Chamber *EH* — 1B **66**
Rider's Rings Enclosures — 1A **16**
Rillaton Barrow — 3A **20**
Robin Hood's Butts — 2C **31**
Roughtor Hut Circles — 2D **19**
St Breock Downs Monolith *EH* — 1B **12**
St Piran's Round (Perran Round) — 2D **11**
Scorhill Stone Circle — 2A **22**
Setta Barrow — 3B **34**
Shovel Down Stone Rows — 2A **22**
Sperris Quoit — 2B **6**
Spinster's Rock Burial Chamber — 1B **22**
Stall Moor Stone Row — 1A **16**
Stannon Stone Circle — 3D **19**
Stripple Stones Henge & Circle — 3D **19**
Tregiffian Burial Chamber *EH* — 3B **6**
Trethevy Quoit *EH* — 1A **14**
Trippet Stones Circle — 3D **19**
Upper Plym Valley Prehistoric Sites *EH* — 1D **15**
Wambarrows — 3C **35**
Zennor Quoit — 2B **6**

Railway (Heritage, Narrow Gauge, Miniature)

Beer Heights Light Railway — 2C **25**
Bickington Steam Railway — 3C **23**
Bicton Woodland Railway, East Budleigh — 2A **24**
Bodmin & Wenford Railway — 1C **13** to 1D **13**
Brean Central Miniature Railway — 1C **37**
Buckfastleigh Miniature Railway — 1B **16**
Combe Martin Wildlife Park Railway — 2D **33**
Cricket St Thomas Railway — 3D **31**
Dartmoor Railway — 1D **21**
Devon Railway Centre — 3D **29**
Dobwalls Miniature Railroad — 1A **14**
Exmoor Steam Railway — 3A **34**
Exmouth Express — 2A **24**
Gorse Blossom Miniature Railway & Woodland Park — 3C **23**
Great Torrington Railway — 2D **27**
Jungle Express, Paignton — 2C **17**
Lappa Valley Steam Railway — 2A **12**
Launceston Steam Railway — 2B **20**
Little Western Railway — Newquay
Lynbarn Railway, The — 1B **26**
Lynton & Lynmouth Cliff Railway — Lynton & Lynmouth

Oddicombe Cliff Railway — 1D **17**
Paignton & Dartmouth Steam Railway — 1C **17** to 2C **17**
Paradise Railway — 2C **7**
Pixieland Miniature Railway — 2A **26**
Plym Valley Railway (Woodland Line) — 2D **15**
Seaton Tramway — 1C **25**
South Devon Railway (Primrose Line) — 1B **16** to 1C **17**
Tamarisk Miniature Railway — 3A **18**
Weston Miniature Railway — 1D **37**
West Somerset Railway — 1B **30** to 2D **35**

Roman Remains

Martinhoe Beacon Roman Fortlet *NT* — 2A **34**
Old Burrow Roman Fortlet — 2B **34**

Spot Height

Brown Willy 420 m (1377 ft) — 3D **19**
Dunkery Beacon 519 m (1704 ft) *NT* — 2C **35**
Golden Cap 191 m (627 ft) — 1D **25**
High Willhays 621 m (2038 ft) — 2D **21**
Pilsdon Pen 277 m (909 ft) *NT* — 3D **31**
Telegraph Hill 51 m (167 ft), St Mary's, Isles of Scilly — 1B **66**
Western Common 493 m (1617 ft) — 3B **34**
Wills Neck 384 m (1260 ft) — 3B **36**

Theme Park

See also Leisure Park

Flambards Village — 3D **7**
Spirit of the West American Theme Park — 1B **12**

Vineyard

See also Cidermaker

Camel Valley Vineyard — 1C **13**
Clawford Vineyard — 3B **26**
Down St Mary Vineyard & Winery — 3B **28**
Highfield Vineyards — 2D **29**
Moorlynch Vineyard — 3D **37**
Polmassick Vineyard — 3B **12**
Porthallow Vineyard & Cider Farm — 2B **8**
Sharpham Vineyard — 2C **17**
Staplecombe Vineyards — 1C **31**
Veryan Vineyard — 3B **12**

Visitor Centre/Information Centre

Axminster Carpets Visitor Centre — 1C **25**
Barbican Glassworks — Plymouth
Berry Head Country Park Visitor Centre, Brixham — 2D **17**
Blackdown Hills Interpretation Centre, Clayhidon — 2B **30**
Boscastle Visitor Centre — 1D **19**
Bude Visitor Centre — Bude
Burrows Centre, Northam — 3C **33**
Cannington Countryside Visitor Centre — 3C **37**
Charmouth Heritage Coast Centre — 1D **25**
Clovelly Centre, The — 1B **26**

Cockington Country Park Visitor Centre — 1C
Cornwall Industrial Discovery Centre, Pool —
Daphne du Maurier Literary Centre, The — Fov
Dawlish Warren Local Nature Reserve Visitor C — 3D **23**
Delabole Wind Farm Renewable Energy Centre — 2C **19**
Eggesford Country Centre — 2A **28**
Fyne Court Visitor Centre — 3C **37**
Gwennap Pit Visitor Centre, St Day — 3D **11**
Hinkley Point Visitor Centre — 2C **37**
Lizard Countryside Centre, The, Garras — 2B
Maunsel Canal Centre — 1D **31**
Meldon Viaduct & Quarry Visitors Centre — 1C
Mineral Tramways Discovery Centre, The, Brea — 1D **7**
Mount Edgcumbe Country Park Information Ce Cremyll — 2C **15**
North Cornwall Wildlife Information Centre, Wadebridge — 3B **18**
Okehampton Station Visitor Centre — 1D **21**
Peat Moors Visitor Centre — 2D **37**
Polzeath Visitor Centre — 3B **18**
Porlock Visitor Centre — 2C **35**
Quantock Information Centre — 3B **36**
Quay House Visitor Centre — Exeter
St Austell Brewery Visitor Centre — 2C **13**
Siblyback Lake Visitor Centre, St Cleer — 3A **2**
Slapton Ley Field Centre — 3C **17**
Somerset Levels & Moors Visitor Centre — 2D
South East Cornwall Discovery Centre — Looe
Stover Country Park Ranger's Office, Heathfield — 3C **23**
Tamar Lakes Water Park Interpretation Centre, Alfardisworthy — 2A **26**
Tarka Trail (Railway Carriage) Visitor Centre, Bideford — 1C **27**
Town & Countryside Centre — Bodmin
Wembury Marine Centre — 3D **15**
West Somerset Railway Visitor Centre, Bishops Lydeard — 1B **30**
Wimbleball Water Park Information Kiosk, Brompton Regis — 3D **35**

Wildlife Park

See also Animal Collection, Farm Park, Zoo

Alstone Wildlife Park — 2D **37**
Combe Martin Wildlife & Dinosaur Park — 2A
Cricket St Thomas Wildlife Park — 3D **31**
Dartmoor Wildlife Park — 2D **15**
Porfell Animal Land Wildlife Park — 2D **13**
Tropiquaria — 2A **36**

Windmill

See also Industrial Monument

Ashton (Chapel Allerton) Towermill — 1D **37**
Stembridge (High Ham) Towermill *NT* — 3D **3**

Zoo/Safari Park

See also Animal Collection, Farm Park, Wildlife

Exmoor Zoological Park — 2A **34**
Newquay Zoo — Newquay
Paignton Zoo Environmental Park — 2C **17**

Every possible care has been taken to ensure that the information given is accurate and whilst the publishers would be grateful to learn of any errors, they regret they cannot accept any responsibility for any loss thereby caused.

Photo credits:
Barnabys Picture Library — Front Cover (Top) St. Ives (bottom) River Fowey; P.1 St Michaels Mount; P.4 North Cornish Coast; P.39 (bottom right) Clovelly
P.41 Brixham; P.44 Exeter Cathedral, Tudor Buildings Exeter; P.45 Dart Valley; P.47 River Fowey; P.55 Padstow Harbour;
P.58 Plymouth Barbican, Drake Island Plymouth; P.59 Smeaton's Tower, The Hoe Plymouth; P.60 St. Ives.

Corbis Images — P.39 (bottom left) Hartland Point, Bryan Pickering; P.40 Cornish Countryside, Andrew Brown; P.42 Coastline Cornwall, Sally A. Morgan;
P.43 River Dart, Patrick Ward; P.49 Ilfracombe, Paul Thompson; P.54 Fore Street, Totnes, Ric Ergenbright; P. 63 Torbay Harbour, Bryan Pickering;
P.64 Bodmin Moor, Andrew Brown; P.65 Portchapel Beach, Adam Woolfit.